Tell Me More

ED. SIMON ADORIAN

Cascades consultants:
John Mannion, Former Head of English, London
Sheena Davies, Principal Teacher, Glasgow
Adrian Jackson, General English Advisor – English, West Sussex
Geoff Fox, Former Senior Lecturer at the University of Exeter
    School of Education, and a National Curriculum Advisor
Emily Rought-Brooks, Head of English, London

ED. SIMON ADORIAN

Tell Me More

An imprint of HarperCollins*Publishers*

Published by HarperCollins*Publishers* Limited
77–85 Fulham Palace Road
Hammersmith
London
W6 8JB

www.**Collins**Education.com
Online support for schools and colleges

Reprinted 10 9 8 7 6 5 4 3 2 1

ISBN: 0 00 711483 4

British Library Cataloguing in Publication Data
A Catalogue record for this publication is available from the British Library

Commissioning editor: Domenica de Rosa
Editor: Gaynor Spry
Cover design: Ken Vail Graphic Design, Cambridge
Typesetting: Derek Lee
Cover photograph/illustration: Chandra at NB Illustration
Production: Katie Morris

Printed and bound by Imago

You might also like to visit
www.**fireandwater**.co.uk
The book lover's website

Contents

Introduction   7

The Voice   9

from *The Pigman*   PAUL ZINDEL   10

from *The Specialist*   CHARLES SALE   14

from *The Genius*   FRANK O'CONNOR   18

from *A Lady of Letters*   ALAN BENNETT   23

from *Paddy Clarke Ha Ha Ha*   RODDY DOYLE   27

Storytellers   32

William's Version   JAN MARK   33

Welsh Incident   ROBERT GRAVES   42

from *A Kestrel for a Knave*   BARRY HINES   46

I Shot the Sheriff   BOB MARLEY   51

The Shah of Blah   SALMAN RUSHDIE   54

Lies   59

The Open Window   SAKI   60

from *This Lime Tree Bower*   CONOR MCPHERSON   66

from *The Tulip Touch*   ANNE FINE   69

Suspense   73

The Monkey's Paw   W.W. JACOBS   74

The Son Murdered by his Parents
     KATHARINE BRIGGS AND RUTH TONGUE   91

Late   CAROL ANN DUFFY   94

An Arrest   AMBROSE BIERCE   97

Reported Horror 101

from *King Oedipus*   SOPHOCLES 102
from *Twenty Four Hours*   MARGARET MAHY 107

A Twist in the Tale 111

The Goat and the Ass   AESOP 111
The Huntsman   EDWARD LOWBURY 113
The Happy Man's Shirt   ITALO CALVINO 116
Bottles   DAVID GREYGOOSE 120
An Aeroplane Journey   JOHN HEGLEY 123
Three Trickster Tales   TRADITIONAL INDIAN, VIETNAMESE
    AND AFRICAN TALES 126

Magical Tales 131

The Fisherman and the Jinnee   ARABIAN NIGHTS 132
Urashima and the Turtle   TRADITIONAL JAPANESE TALE 137

The Moral of the Story 140

Samurai and Hakuin   TRADITIONAL ZEN BUDDHIST TALE 141
Parable of the Vineyard Labourers   MATTHEW 20 v.1–16 143
from *Julius Caesar*   WILLIAM SHAKESPEARE 146

Modern Day Myths 149

In the Back Seat   KEVIN CROSSLEY-HOLLAND 150
Rain Man   YORICK BROWN AND MIKE FLYNN 151

The Structure of the Stories 153
Activities Mapping: English Framework Objectives Grid 158
Acknowledgements 162
Other Cascades Titles 166

Introduction

'The Arabian Nights' is the story of a bitter king who kills all his brides the day after he marries them. One day he marries a clever young woman called Scheherazade. On their wedding night she starts to tell a series of intricately interwoven tales (sometimes stories within stories within stories). Scheherazade's plan is for the King to become so involved in her never-ending tales that he will keep putting off the day of her execution.

People always have and always will tell one another stories. The gossip, the comedian, the reporter and the fiction writer are all tapping into other people's appetite for tales.

The oral tradition of passing on stories exists in every culture and, before writing or printing began, the storyteller was an admired member of the community. Where once people would travel to hear folk stories, we might now read books, watch television or visit cinemas. To some extent, we think and learn in stories: tales of fantasy can represent our dreams or show us ways that our fears and problems can be solved. When we pass on anecdotes, jokes and gossip, we often reshape them, leaving bits out here, polishing and adding detail there, and this helps us to make sense of what is going on around us. The power of stories to entertain, to mystify and to teach is as strong today as it ever was – even if the media are different.

Stories also allow us to pass on and understand our history: of our nation, of our community and of our family. Salman Rushdie, one of the modern writers included in this anthology, said: "Every family has stories about itself. You could argue, in fact, that the collection of stories a family has about itself is actually the definition of a family. When someone joins a family – a child is born, someone marries into it – they are gradually told all the secret family stories. And when you finally know all the stories, you belong to the family."

The stories in this collection are drawn from a range of cultures and sources – some from oral storytelling traditions, others from authors who have woven tales into their writing. Each section of the anthology has been designed to explore a specific element of the art of storytelling through different texts and supporting activities.

And Scheherazade's scheme to avoid her death with a never-ending run of tales? Well, that's another story ...

The Voice

"I believe it is the easiest thing in the world to tell a story –
and the hardest to be a fine storyteller."
Ruth Sawyer, *The Way of the Storyteller*

"The tale is not beautiful if nothing is added to it."
Italian proverb

"It's the way I tell 'em."
Frank Carson, Irish comedian

from *The Pigman*

Paul Zindel

Paul Zindel's 1968 novel *The Pigman* is told by dual narrators – a teenage boy and girl called John and Lorraine. They give their versions of the traumatic events arising from their relationship with an eccentric old man.

Paul Zindel has written, "I like storytelling. We all have one thing that we do that gives us self-esteem, that makes us proud; it's necessary. I have to tell stories because that's the way the wiring went in."

John, the writer of this chapter, is a narrator with plenty of attitude.

I suppose it all started when Lorraine and I and these two amoebae[1] called Dennis Kobin and Norton Kelly were hot on these phone gags last September. We did the usual ones like dialling any number out of the book and asking, "Is your refrigerator running?"

"Yes."

"Go catch it then."

And we called every drugstore.

"Do you have Prince Albert in a can?"

"Yes."

"Then let him out."

But then we made up a new game in which the object was to keep a stranger talking on the phone as long as

---

[1] **amoebae:** single-celled organisms

possible. At least twice a week we'd meet for a telephone marathon. Wednesday afternoons we'd have it at Dennis's house because his mother goes shopping at the supermarket and his father doesn't get home from work until after 6 p.m., even when he's sober. And on Sundays we'd do it at Norton's because his father plays golf and his mother is so retarded she doesn't know what's coming off anyway, but at least they didn't mind if their kids used the house. Mine and Lorraine's we can't even go to. We couldn't use the phone at Lorraine's anyway because her mother doesn't have unlimited service, and at my house my mother is a disinfectant fanatic. She would have gotten too nervous over all of us using her purified instrument. Another difficulty there is that my father, whom I warmly refer to as Bore, put a lock on our phone – one of those round locks you put in the first dialhole so you can't dial. He put it on because of a little exchange we had when he called from work.

"Do you realize I've been trying to get your mother for an hour and a half and the line's been busy?" Bore bellowed.

"Those things happen. I was talking to a friend."

"If you don't use the phone properly, I'm going to put a lock on it."

"Yeah? No kidding?"

Now it was just the way I said *yeah* that set him off, and that night when we got home, he just put the lock on the phone and didn't say a word. But I'm used to it. Bore and I have been having a lot of trouble communicating lately as it is, and sometimes I go a little crazy when I feel I'm being picked on or not being trusted. That's why I finally put airplane glue in the keyhole of the lock so nobody could use the telephone, key or no key.

Anyway, the idea of a telephone marathon was you had to close your eyes and stick your finger on a number in the directory and then call it up to see how long you could keep whoever answered talking on the phone. I wasn't too good at this because I used to burst out laughing. The only thing I could do that kept them talking a while before they hung up was to tell them I was calling from *TV Quiz* and that they had won a prize. That was always good for three and a half minutes before they caught on.

The longest anyone ever lasted was Dennis, because he picked out this old woman who lived alone and was desperate to talk to anyone. Dennis is really not very bright. In fact, he talks so slowly some people think he has brain damage. But he told this woman he had called her number because he had heard she gave good advice and his problem was that he was about to die from a hideous skin disease because a rat had bitten off his nose when he was a baby and the skin grafts[2] didn't take. He kept her on the phone for two hours and twenty-six minutes. That was the record!

Now Lorraine can blame all the other things on me, but she was the one who picked out the Pigman's phone number. If you ask me, I think he would have died anyway. Maybe we speeded things up a little, but you can't really say we murdered him.

Not murdered him.

---

[2] **skin grafts:** skin moved from an undamaged area to the damaged area

Activities

Reading

1 This chapter establishes some of the novel's characters and also John's attitude to them. In the first sentence John describes two close friends as 'amoebae'. Make a list of other insulting terms used by John to describe friends and family.

2 What picture does John give of his home life?

3 Read the last two paragraphs carefully. What do you expect to find out in the rest of the novel?

Speaking and listening

4 Discuss whether you think the writer means us to like and trust John.

5 Work with a partner to role-play one of the telephone marathons. Prepare two versions of the same conversation: one where the dialler keeps the stranger talking for a long time; one where they are less successful.

Language study

'Sometimes I go *a little* crazy.'

'I wasn't *too good* at this.'

'Dennis is *really not very* bright.'

6 What is the effect of the words in italics?

7 John refers to his rows with his father as 'a little exchange' and 'having trouble communicating'. Invent other ironic terms for describing conflicts.

Writing

8 '... you can't really say we murdered him. Not murdered him.' The chapter ends with a deliberate 'hook' to catch the reader. To find out more about John's involvement in a possible murder, we would have to read on. Write your own opening chapter using, as in *The Pigman*, the first person (for example, 'I suppose it all started when ...') and describing some details of the narrator's life (for example, a story from home, school or work), and end with a 'hook'.

9 Write an account of the argument between John and his father about the use of the telephone. Write from the father's point of view. Choose words that make the father's attitude very clear.

Further reading

Other books you might like to read in full are *The Pigman* and *The Pigman's Legacy*, both by Paul Zindel.

from *The Specialist*

Charles Sale

Charles 'Chic' Sale was an American actor and stand-up comedian. In 1929 he wrote *The Specialist*, a short book based on material from his stage act, which has since become a comic classic. The narrator, Lem Putt, is a specialist builder of privies (outside lavatories) in a remote country area of the USA. In the book he passes on the secrets of his art and his deep thoughts about many aspects of life. Here he considers the best way to paint your privy.

"You need contrast – just like they use on them railroad crossin' bars – so you can see 'em in the dark."

"If I was you, I'd paint her a bright red, with white trimmin's – just like your barn. Then she'll match up nice in the daytime, and you can spot 'er easy at night, when you ain't got much time to go scoutin' around.

"There's a lot of fine points to puttin' up a first-class privy[1] that the average man don't think about. It's no job for an amachoor, take my word on it. There's a whole lot more to it than you can see by just takin' a few squints at your nabor's. Why, one of the worst tragedies around heer in years was because old man Clark's boys thought they knowed somethin' about this kind of work, and they didn't.

"Old man Clark – if he's a day he's ninety-seven – lives over there across the holler with his boys. Asked me to

---

[1] *privy:* outside toilet

come over and estimate on their job. My price was too high; so they decided to do it themselves. And that's where the trouble begun.

"I was doin' a little paper hangin' at the time for that widder that lives down past the old creamery. As I'd drive by I could see the boys a-workin'. Of course, I didn't want to butt in, so used to just holler at 'em on the way by and say, naborly like: 'Hey, boys, see you're doin a little buildin'.' You see, I didn't want to act like I was buttin' in on their work; but I knowed all the time they was going to have trouble with that privy. As they did. From all outside appearance it was a regulation job, but not being experienced along this line, they didn't anchor her.

"You see, I put a 4 by 4 that runs from the top right straight on down five foot into the ground. That's why you never see any of my jobs upset Hallowe'en night. They might *pull* 'em out, but they'll never upset 'em.

"Here's what happened: They didn' anchor theirs, and they painted it solid red – two bad mistakes.

"Hallowe'en night came along, darker than pitch. Old man Clark was out in there. Some of them devilish nabor boys was out for no good, and they upset 'er with the old man in it.

"Of course, the old man got to callin' and his boys heard the noise. One of 'em sez: 'What's the racket? Somebody must be at the chickens.' So they took the lantern, started out to the chicken shed. They didn't find anything wrong there, and they started back to the house. Then they heerd the dog bark, and one of his boys sez: 'Sounds like that barkin' is over towards the privy.' It bein' painted red, they couldn't see she was upset, so they started over there.

"In the meantime the old man had gotten so confused that he started to crawl out through the hole, yellin' for help all the time. The boys reckonized his voice and come runnin', but just as they got there he lost his holt and fell. After that they just *called* – didn't go near him. So you see what a tragedy that was; and they tell me he has been practically ostercized[2] from society since."

---

[2] **ostercized:** ostracized – ignored by everyone

Activities

Reading

1 Lem Putt describes this event as 'one of the worst tragedies around heer in years'. What does that tell us about life 'around heer'?

2 How can we tell that Lem thinks of himself as an 'expert'?

Speaking and listening

3 In groups, discuss any storytellers and comedians you know of who do not use standard English. Why do you think jokes and stories often work better in local accents and dialects?

4 Try a role-play activity around the extract. After this disaster Mr Clark has been 'practically ostercized from society since'. Improvise a conversation about the Hallowe'en night disaster between other villagers. Try to include some features of the country dialect.

Language study

5 *The Specialist* is told in a local dialect and the author has used unusual spellings to convey Lem's accent, for example, 'heer' for 'here'. Make a list of other non-standard spellings in the text.

6 The tale is told in local dialect with its non-standard verb forms (such as 'they ain't', 'they knowed'). Collect some examples of non-standard verb forms in your own local dialect.

Writing

7 Write a formal police statement giving an account of Mr Clark's Hallowe'en disaster. The account will need to establish what happened and why. (Useful connectives to explain cause and effect are: '... because ...', '... therefore ...', '... as a result of this ...', '... due to ...', '... owing to ...').

Compare and contrast

8 Compare this extract with the story of the taddies from *A Kestrel for a Knave* on page 46, told in local dialect by a boy from Yorkshire. Choose an extract to read aloud from each piece. As part of your presentation, explain some key features of each dialect.

Further reading

You might like to read the complete text of *The Specialist* by Charles Sale Other examples of dialect writing include *Me Rememba Sweet Jamaica* by Andrea Sakinah Reynolds and Louise Bennett Coverly, and *Poems, Chiefly in the Scottish Dialect* by Robert Burns.

from *The Genius*

Frank O'Connor

Frank O'Connor (1903–66) wrote plays, novels and critical works, but he is best known for his short stories, often set in his native town of Cork. In *The Genius*, the narrator looks back on a childhood where he never quite fitted in.

Some kids are cissies by nature but I was a cissy by conviction. Mother had told me about geniuses; I wanted to be one, and I could see for myself that fighting, as well as being sinful, was dangerous. The kids round the Barrack where I lived were always fighting. Mother said they were savages, that I needed proper friends, and that once I was old enough to go to school I would meet them.

My way, when someone wanted to fight and I could not get away, was to climb on the nearest wall and argue like hell in a shrill voice about Our Blessed Lord and good manners. This was a way of attracting attention, and it usually worked because the enemy, having stared incredulously[1] at me for several minutes, wondering if he would have time to hammer my head on the pavement before someone came out to him, yelled something like 'blooming cissy' and went away in disgust. I didn't like being called a cissy but I preferred it to fighting. I felt very like one of those poor mongrels who slunk through our

---

[1] *incredulously:* disbelievingly

neighbourhood and took to their heels when anyone came near them, and I always tried to make friends with them.

I toyed with games, and enjoyed kicking a ball gently before me along the pavement till I discovered that any boy who joined me grew violent and started to shoulder me out of the way. I preferred little girls because they didn't fight so much, but otherwise I found them insipid and lacking in any solid basis of information. The only women I cared for were grown-ups, and my most intimate[2] friend was an old washerwoman called Miss Cooney who had been in the lunatic asylum and was very religious. It was she who had told me all about dogs. She would run a mile after anyone she saw hurting an animal, and even went to the police about them, but the police knew she was mad and paid no attention.

She was a sad-looking woman with grey hair, high cheekbones and toothless gums. While she ironed, I would sit for hours in the hot, steaming, damp kitchen, turning over the pages of her religious books. She was fond of me too, and told me she was sure I would be a priest. I agreed that I might be a bishop, but she didn't seem to think so highly of bishops. I told her there were so many other things I might be that I couldn't make up my mind, but she only smiled at this. Miss Cooney thought there was only one thing a genius could be and that was a priest.

On the whole I thought an explorer was what I would be. Our house was in a square between two roads, one terraced above the other, and I could leave home, follow the upper road for a mile past the Barrack, turn left on any of the

---

[2] *intimate:* best, closest

intervening roads and lanes, and return almost without leaving the pavement. It was astonishing what valuable information you could pick up on a trip like that. When I came home I wrote down my adventures in a book called *The Voyages of Johnson Martin*, 'with many Maps and Illustrations, Irishtown University Press, 3s. 6d. nett'. I was also compiling *The Irishtown University Song Book for Use in Schools and Institutions by Johnson Martin,* which had the words and music of my favourite songs. I could not read music yet but I copied it from anything that came handy, preferring staff to solfa[3] because it looked better on the page. But I still wasn't sure what I would be. All I knew was that I intended to be famous and have a statue put up to me near that of Father Matthew, in Patrick Street. Father Matthew was called the Apostle of Temperance,[4] but I didn't think much of temperance. So far our town hadn't a proper genius and I intended to supply the deficiency.

But my work continued to bring home to me the great gaps in my knowledge. Mother understood my difficulty and worried herself endlessly finding answers to my questions, but neither she nor Miss Cooney had a great store of the sort of information I needed, and Father was more a hindrance than a help. He was talkative enough about subjects that interested himself but they did not greatly interest me. "Ballybeg," he would say brightly. "Market town. Population 648. Nearest station, Rathkeale." He was also forthcoming enough about other things, but later, Mother would take me aside and explain that he was

---

[3] **solfa:** a way of teaching music
[4] **temperance:** avoidance of alcohol

only joking again. This made me mad, because I never knew when he was joking and when he wasn't.

I can see now, of course, that he didn't really like me. It was not the poor man's fault. He had never expected to be the father of a genius and it filled him with forebodings.[5] He looked round at all his contemporaries who had normal, bloodthirsty, illiterate children, and shuddered at the thought that I would never be good for anything but being a genius. To give him his due, it wasn't himself he worried about, but there had never been anything like it in the family before and he dreaded the shame of it.

---

[5] *forebodings:* dread

Activities

Reading

1 The narrator, Johnson Martin, considers himself a genius. What problems does this cause him? What problems does this cause his family and neighbours?

2 Why does the child befriend 'poor mongrels' and 'mad' Miss Cooney?

3 Collect two sets of quotations from the text which:
   ● encourage us to feel sympathy for Johnson
   ● encourage us to laugh at him.

Speaking and listening

4 Johnson Martin says, 'All I knew was that I intended to be famous.' Many famous writers and performers have also written about the trouble they had 'fitting in' with other children. In pairs or small groups, discuss why you think that is.

5 Prepare a dialogue between young Johnson 'the genius' and adult Johnson the narrator/writer. The adult can challenge the child about his behaviour and attitudes. (This could be prepared as a solo or paired piece.)

Writing

6 'Some kids are cissies by nature but I was a cissy by conviction.' Write a funny first-person account in which an older narrator looks back humorously at the way they were as a child. For example: The main reason I had no friends as a young child was ...

   The statement could then be followed by anecdotes that support it.

Compare and contrast

7 Now read the extract from Roddy Doyle's *Paddy Clarke Ha Ha Ha* on page 27. Compare the way the two authors:
   ● create the voices and characters of their narrators
   ● portray childhood in an Irish town.
   What are the key differences and similarities?

Further reading

You might like to read *My Oedipus Complex and Other Stories* by Frank O'Connor and *Angela's Ashes* by Frank McCourt (also available on video) which gives a different autobiographical account of an Irish childhood.

from *A Lady of Letters*

Alan Bennett

Alan Bennett (born 1934) began writing and performing comedy in revue shows, including *Beyond the Fringe*. He has written many plays for the stage, radio and television as well as the screenplay for the film *The Madness of King George*. Collections of his stories, diaries and essays have also been published.

Alan Bennett's *Talking Heads* monologues were originally written for television and were first broadcast in 1987. In *A Lady of Letters*, Miss Ruddock gives an account of a campaign of hate mail towards a neighbour that eventually leads to her arrest.

THINKING about it afterwards, I realized it must have been the doctor that alerted the vicar. Came round anyway. Not the old vicar. I'd have known him. This was a young fellow in a collar and tie, could have been anybody. I didn't take the chain off. I said, "How do I know you're the vicar, have you any identification?" He shoves a little cross round the door. I said, "What's this?" He said, "A cross." I said, "A cross doesn't mean anything. Youths wear crosses nowadays. Hooligans. They wear crosses in their ears." He said, "Not like this. This is a real cross. A working cross. It's the tool of my trade." I was still a bit dubious,[1] then I saw he had cycle clips on so I let him in.

---

[1] *dubious:* doubtful

He chats for a bit, this and that, no mention of God for long enough. They keep him up their sleeve for as long as they can, vicars, they know it puts people off. Went through a long rigmarole about love. How love comes in different forms ... loving friends, loving the countryside, loving music. People would be surprised to learn, he said (and I thought, "Here we go"), people would be surprised to learn that they loved God all the time and just didn't know it. I cut him short. I said, "If you've come round here to talk about God you're barking up the wrong tree. I'm an atheist." He was a bit stumped. I could see. They don't expect you to be an atheist[2] when you're a miss. Vicars, they think if you're a single person they're on a good wicket. He said, "Well, Miss Ruddock, I shall call again. I shall look on you as a challenge."

He hadn't been gone long when there's another knock, only this time it's a policeman, with a woman policeman in tow. Ask if they can come in and have a word. I said, "What for?" He said, "You know what for." I said, "I don't," but I let them in. Takes his helmet off, only young and says he'll come straight to the point: was it me who'd been writing these letters? I said, "What letters? I don't write letters." He said, "Letters." I said, "Everyone writes letters. I bet you write letters." He said, "Not like you, love." I said, "Don't love me. You'd better give me your name and number. I intend to write to your superintendent."

It turns out it's to do with the couple opposite. I said, "Well, why are you asking me?" He said, "We're asking you because who was it wrote to the chemist saying his wife was a prostitute? We're asking you because who was it gave

---

[2] **atheist:** a person who doesn't believe in God

the lollipop man a nervous breakdown?" I said, "Well, he was interfering with those children." He said, "The court bound you over to keep the peace. This is a serious matter." I said, "It is a serious matter. I can't keep the peace when there's cruelty and neglect going on under my nose. I shouldn't keep the peace when there's a child suffering. It's not my duty to keep the peace then, is it?" So then madam takes over, the understanding approach. She said didn't I appreciate this was a caring young couple? I said if they were a caring young couple why did you never see the kiddy? If they were a caring young couple why did they go gadding off every night, leaving the kiddy alone in the house? She said because the kiddy wasn't alone in the house. The kiddy wasn't in the house. The kiddy was in hospital in Bradford, that's where they were going every night. And that's where the kiddy died, last Friday. I said, "What of? Neglect?" She said, "No. Leukaemia."[3]

Pause.

He said, "You'd better get your hat and coat on."

---

[3] **leukaemia:** cancer of the blood

Activities

Reading

1 What is Miss Ruddock's attitude to the vicar and the police officers?

2 What kind of letters has Miss Ruddock been writing?

3 Why do you think the policeman asks Miss Ruddock to put on her hat and coat? What do you think will happen after this interview?

Speaking and listening

4 Prepare a reading of the last two paragraphs (starting 'It turns out'), discussing the best way to read the different voices. Note also the pause before the last sentence.

Language study

5 Look at 'I said' (line 5) and 'He shoves' (line 6). Notice how the narrative slips from the past to the present tense, as people do when they tell anecdotes. Find three other examples in this extract where the speaker uses the present tense to recount a past event. Why do you think the author chose this style?

6 'Came round anyway.' This is an example of a short, simple sentence. Find some other examples. What is the effect of these sentences when you read the piece aloud?

Writing

7 Miss Ruddock's case will eventually come to court. Write a speech to defend or prosecute her as she is charged with harassment.

8 Write a monologue in which the speaker reveals an important event in their past. Before writing, consider:
   ● the character and their 'story' (make a brief timeline)
   ● the setting (somewhere on their own, waiting to meet someone; at a bus stop; cooking).
   When you write, aim to 'jumble up' the details of today (such as the bus they're waiting for) and the past (for example, the main story). Try to use plenty of short sentences and to mix tenses. One possible starting point could be: Thinking about it afterwards, I realized it must have been ...

9 Perform or read the monologue.

Further reading

You might like to read *The Complete Talking Heads* by Alan Bennett, which is also available on BBC audiotape and video; and *Solo 1, 2, 3* – a series of monologues for Drama in English by John Goodwin and Bill Taylor.

from *Paddy Clarke Ha Ha Ha*

Roddy Doyle

Roddy Doyle has enjoyed huge success with his novels of contemporary Irish life; *The Commitments*, *The Snapper* and *The Van* have all been adapted as films. His writing is characterized by its energy and sense of humour. This extract comes from his 1993 Booker Prize-winning novel, *Paddy Clarke Ha Ha Ha*. It recounts childhood memories in a voice that imitates the fresh exuberance of a young child.

MISTER Hanley was always in his garden, picking up things, bits of leaf, slugs – he picked them up with his hand; I saw him. His bare hands. He was always digging, leaning in near the wall. I saw a hand when I was going to the shops, Mister Hanley's hand, on the wall, holding himself up as he dug; only his hand. I tried to get past before he stood up, but I couldn't run – I could only walk fast. I wasn't trying not to let him see me; I wasn't scared of him; I just did it. He didn't know I was doing it. I once saw him lying down in the front garden, on his back. His feet were in the flower bed. I waited to see if he was dead; then I was afraid someone was looking at me through the window. When I came back Mister Hanley was gone. He didn't have a job.

– Why not?

– He's retired, said my ma.

– Why is he?

That was why he had the best garden in Barrytown and that was why invading the Hanleys' garden was the biggest dare of all. And that was why the Grand National ended there. Over the hedge, up, through the gate, the winner. Liam hadn't been winning.

In a way, winning was easiest. The winner was the first out onto the path. Mister Hanley couldn't get you there, or his sons, Billy and Laurence. It was the ones that came over the hedge last that were in the biggest danger. Mister Hanley just gave out and spits flew out of his mouth; there was always white stuff in the corners. A lot of old people had mouths like that. Billy Hanley and especially Laurence Hanley killed you if they got you.

– It's about time those two slobs went and got married or something.

– Who'd have them?

Laurence Hanley was fat but he was fast. He grabbed us by the hair. He was the only person I knew who did that. It was weird, a man grabbing people by the hair. He did it because he was fat and couldn't fight properly. He was evil as well. His fingers were stiff and like daggers, much worse than a punch. Four stabs on the side of your chest, while he was holding you up straight with your hair.

– Get out of our garden.

One more for good measure, then he let go.

– Now – stay out!

Sometimes he kicked but he couldn't get his leg up far. He sweated through his trousers.

There were ten fences in the Grand National. All the walls of the front gardens were the same height, the exact same, but the hedges and the trees made them different. And the gardens between the fences, we had to charge across them; pushing was allowed in the gardens, but not pulling or tripping. It was mad; it was brilliant. We started in Ian McEvoy's garden, a straight line for us. There was no handicapping;[1] no one was allowed to start in front of the rest. No one would have wanted it anyway, because you needed a good run at the first wall and no one was going to stand in the next garden alone, waiting for the race to start. It was Byrne's. Missis Byrne had a black lens in her glasses. Specky Three Eyes she was called, but that was the only funny thing about her.

It always took ages for the straight line to get really straight. There was always a bit of shoving; it was allowed, as long as the elbows didn't go up too far, over the neck.

– They're under starter's orders – , said Aidan.

We crept forward. Anyone caught behind the group when the race started could never win and would probably be the one caught by Laurence Hanley.

– They're off!

Aidan didn't do any more commentating after that.

The first fence was easy. McEvoy's wall into Byrne's. There was no hedge. You just had to make sure that you had enough room to swing your legs. Some of us could swing right over without our legs touching the top of the wall – I could – but you needed loads of space for that. Across Byrne's. Screaming and shouting. That was part of it. Trying to get the ones at the back caught. Off the grass, over the flower bed, across the path, over the wall – a hedge. Jump up on the wall, grip the hedge, stand up straight, jump over, down. Danger, danger. Murphy's. Loads of flowers. Kick some of them. Around the car. Hedge before the wall. Foot on the bumper, jump. Land on the hedge,

---

[1] **handicapping:** advantages or disadvantages given to a competitor

roll. Our house. Around the car, no hedge, over the wall. No more screaming; no breath for it. Neck itchy from the hedge. Two more big hedges.

Once, Mister McLoughlin had been cutting the grass when we all came over the hedge, and he nearly had a heart attack.

Up onto Hanley's wall, hold the hedge. Legs straight; it was harder now, really tired. Jump the hedge, roll, up and out their gate.

Winner.

Activities

Reading
1 How do you think local families reacted to this wild street game?
2 'Screaming and shouting. That was part of it. Trying to get the ones at the back caught.' What does this tell us about the game and the children that played it?
3 Look closely at the way the narrator, Paddy Clarke, describes the Hanley family. Why do you think he includes so many unkind details?

Language study
4 Read the last paragraphs from, '– They're off!' Find examples of very short sentences. What effect do they have on the mood of the piece?

Writing
5 Write a first-person account (fiction or non-fiction) of a childhood dare. Like Roddy Doyle, try to tell it through the eyes of the child and to capture the mood of the moment. Aim to use some of the narrative devices seen in this extract, such as:
   ● exact details of the dare
   ● the speech of the people involved
   ● shortened sentences towards the climax.
6 Write a set of rules for the 'Grand National' game. They will need to include:
   ● details of the course
   ● rules about behaviour
   ● guidelines about tactics.
   Try to write them in a humorous style.

Compare and contrast
7 Read this extract alongside the extracts from *The Genius* (page 18) and *This Lime Tree Bower* (page 66). All three are by Irish writers reflecting on their youth. Can you spot any similarities in the way they tell their stories?

Further reading

You might like to read in full *Paddy Clarke Ha Ha Ha* by Roddy Doyle and *Portrait of the Artist as a Young Man* by James Joyce – another example of a famous Irish autobiographical novel.

Storytellers

"A tale never loses in the telling."

Proverb

"The first law of storytelling: 'Every man is bound to leave a story better than he found it.'"

Mary Ward, *Robert Elsmere*

William's Version

Jan Mark

Jan Mark has been writing short stories and novels for children and teenagers since the 1970s, and has won numerous awards for her books. *William's Version* is taken from her 1980 collection, *Nothing To Be Afraid Of*.

WILLIAM and Granny were left to entertain each other for an hour while William's mother went to the clinic.

"Sing to me," said William.

"Granny's too old to sing," said Granny.

"I'll sing to you, then," said William. William only knew one song. He had forgotten the words and the tune, but he sang it several times, anyway.

"Shall we do something else now?" said Granny.

"Tell me a story," said William. "Tell me about the wolf."

"Red Riding Hood?"

"No, not *that* wolf, the other wolf."

"Peter and the wolf?" said Granny.

"Mummy's going to have a baby," said William.

"I know," said Granny.

William looked suspicious.

"How do you know?"

"Well ... she told me. And it shows, doesn't it?"

"The lady down the road had a baby. It looks like a pig," said William. He counted on his fingers. "Three babies looks like three pigs."

"Ah," said Granny. "Once upon a time there were three little pigs. Their names were – "

"They didn't have names," said William.

"Yes they did. The first pig was called – "

"Pigs don't have names."

"Some do. These pigs had names."

"No they didn't." William slid off Granny's lap and went to open the corner cupboard by the fireplace. Old magazines cascaded[1] out as old magazines do when they have been flung into a cupboard and the door slammed shut. He rooted among them until he found a little book covered with brown paper, climbed into the cupboard, opened the book, closed it again and climbed out again. "They didn't have names," he said.

"I didn't know you could read," said Granny, properly impressed.

"C – A – T, wheelbarrow," said William.

"Is that the book Mummy reads to you out of?"

"It's my book," said William.

"But it's the one Mummy reads?"

"If she says please," said William.

"Well, that's Mummy's story, then. My pigs have names."

"They're the wrong pigs," William was not open to negotiation.[2] "I don't want them in this story."

"Can't we have different pigs this time?"

"No. They won't know what to do."

"Once upon a time," said Granny, "there were three little pigs who lived with their mother."

"Their mother was dead," said William.

---

[1] *cascaded:* fell
[2] *negotiation:* debate

"Oh, I'm sure she wasn't," said Granny.

"She was dead. You make bacon out of dead pigs. She got eaten for breakfast and they threw the rind out for the birds."

"So the three little pigs had to find homes for themselves."

"No." William consulted his book. "They had to build little houses."

"I'm just coming to that."

"You said they had to *find* homes. They didn't *find* them."

"The first little pig walked along for a bit until he met a man with a load of hay."

"It was a lady."

"A lady with a load of hay?"

"NO! It was a lady-pig. You said *he*."

"I thought all the pigs were little boy-pigs," said Granny.

"It says lady-pig here," said William. "It says the lady-pig went for a walk and met a man with a load of hay."

"So the lady-pig," said Granny, "said to the man, 'May I have some of that hay to build a house?' and the man said, 'Yes.' Is that right?"

"Yes," said William. "You know that baby?"

"What baby?"

"The one Mummy's going to have. Will that baby have shoes on when it comes out?"

"I don't think so," said Granny.

"It will have cold feet," said William.

"Oh no," said Granny. "Mummy will wrap it up in a soft shawl, all snug."

"I don't *mind* if it has cold feet," William explained. "Go on about the lady-pig."

"So the little lady-pig took the hay and built a little house. Soon the wolf came along and the wolf said – "

"You didn't tell where the wolf lived."

"I don't know where the wolf lived."

"15 Tennyson Avenue, next to the bomb-site," said William.

"I bet it doesn't say that in the book," said Granny, with spirit.

"Yes it does."

"Let me see, then."

William folded himself up with his back to Granny, and pushed the book up under his pullover.

"*I* don't think it says that in the book," said Granny.

"It's in ever so small words," said William.

"So the wolf said, 'Little pig, little pig, let me come in,' and the little pig answered, 'No'. So the wolf said, 'Then I'll huff and I'll puff and I'll blow your house down,' and he huffed and he puffed and he blew the house down, and the little pig ran away."

"He ate the little pig," said William.

"No, no," said Granny. "The little pig ran away."

"He ate the little pig. He ate her in a sandwich."

"All right, he ate the little pig in a sandwich. So the second little pig – "

"You didn't tell about the tricycle."

"What about the tricycle?"

"The wolf got on his tricycle and went to the bread shop to buy some bread. To make the sandwich," William explained, patiently.

"Oh well, the wolf got on his tricycle and went to the bread shop to buy some bread. And he went to the grocer's to buy some butter." This innovation did not go down well.

"He already had some butter in the cupboard," said William.

"So then the second little pig went for a walk and met a man with a load of wood, and the little pig said to the man, 'May I have some of that wood to build a house?' and the man said, 'Yes.'"

"He didn't say please."

"'Please may I have some of that wood to build a house?'"

"It was sticks."

"Sticks *are* wood."

William took out his book and turned the pages. "That's right," he said.

"Why don't you tell the story?" said Granny.

"I can't remember it," said William.

"You could read it out of your book."

"I've lost it," said William, clutching his pullover. "Look, do you know who this is?" He pulled a green angora[3] scarf from under the sofa.

"No, who is it?" said Granny, glad of the diversion.

"This is Doctor Snake." He made the scarf wriggle across the carpet.

"Why is he a doctor?"

"Because he is all furry," said William. He wrapped the doctor round his neck and sat sucking the loose end. "Go on about the wolf."

"So the little pig built a house of sticks and along came the wolf – on his tricycle?"

"He came by bus. He didn't have any money for a ticket so he ate up the conductor."

---

[3] *angora:* goat-hair

"That wasn't very nice of him," said Granny.

"No," said William. "It wasn't *very* nice.

"And the wolf said, 'Little pig, little pig, let me come in,' and the little pig said, 'No,' and the wolf said, 'Then I'll huff and I'll puff and I'll blow your house down,' so he huffed and he puffed and he blew the house down. And then what did he do?" Granny asked, cautiously.

William was silent.

"Did he eat the second little pig?"

"Yes."

"How did he eat this little pig?" said Granny, prepared for more pig sandwiches or possibly pig on toast.

"With his mouth," said William.

"Now the third little pig went for a walk and met a man with a load of bricks. And the little pig said, '*Please* may I have some of those bricks to build a house?' and the man said, 'Yes.' So the little pig took the bricks and built a house."

"He built it on the bomb-site."

"Next door to the wolf?" said Granny. "That was very silly of him."

"There wasn't anywhere else," said William. "All the roads were full up."

"The wolf didn't have to come by bus or tricycle this time, then, did he?" said Granny, grown cunning.

"Yes." William took out the book and peered in, secretively. "He was playing in the cemetery. He had to get another bus."

"And did he eat the conductor this time?"

"No. A nice man gave him some money, so he bought a ticket."

"I'm glad to hear it," said Granny.

"He ate the nice man," said William.

"So the wolf got off the bus and went up to the little pig's house, and he said, 'Little pig, little pig, let me come in,' and the little pig said, 'No,' and then the wolf said, 'I'll huff and I'll puff and I'll blow your house down,' and he huffed and he puffed and he huffed and he puffed but he couldn't blow the house down because it was made of bricks."

"He couldn't blow it down," said William, "because it was stuck to the ground."

"Well, anyway, the wolf got very cross then, and he climbed on the roof and shouted down the chimney, 'I'm coming to get you!' but the little pig just laughed and put a big saucepan of water on the fire."

"He put it on the gas stove."

"He put it on the *fire*," said Granny, speaking very rapidly, "and the wolf fell down the chimney and into the pan of water and was boiled and the little pig ate him for supper."

William threw himself full length on the carpet and screamed.

"He didn't! He didn't! *He didn't*! He didn't eat the wolf."

Granny picked him up, all stiff and kicking, and sat him on her lap.

"Did I get it wrong again, love? Don't cry. Tell me what really happened."

William wept, and wiped his nose on Doctor Snake.

"The little pig put the saucepan on the gas stove and the wolf got down the chimney and put the little pig in the saucepan and boiled him. He had him for tea, with chips," said William.

"Oh," said Granny. "I've got it all wrong, haven't I? Can I see the book, then I shall know, next time."

William took the book from under his pullover. Granny opened it and read, *First Aid for Beginners: a Practical Handbook.*

"I see," said Granny. "I don't think I can read this. I left my glasses at home. You can tell Gran how it ends."

William turned to the last page which showed a prostrate man with his leg in a splint; *compound fracture*[4] *of the femur.*[5]

"Then the wolf washed up and got on his tricycle and went to see his Granny, and his Granny opened the door and said, 'Hello, William!'"

"I thought it was the wolf."

"It was. It was the wolf. His name was William Wolf," said William.

"What a nice story," said Granny. "You tell it much better than I do."

"I can see up your nose," said William. "It's all whiskery."

---

[4] *compound fracture:* break in the bone through the skin
[5] *femur:* leg bone

Activities

Reading

1   Draw up two lists to show the different features of William's and Granny's version of *The Three Little Pigs*. For example:

William's version	*Granny's version*
Pigs had no names	Pigs had names
Mother pig eaten for breakfast	Mother lived with the pigs

2   Why do you think William needed to have his own version of the story?

3   Why does William look at the First Aid book to back up his version?

Speaking and listening

4   Work with a partner to present a conversation between an adult and a young child. The adult is telling or reading a traditional tale which the child wants to adapt.

5   Work in threes to prepare a reading of *William's Version* using different voices for the story, and for William and Granny. Pay close attention to the way the dialogue is set out and punctuated so that your reading is effective. Then present or record your reading.

6   This story relies heavily on dialogue. Taking just the beginning of the story on page 33, try rewriting it as reported speech rather than direct speech. Discuss the different effects achieved by each version.

Writing

7   Use your drama work (see Speaking and listening above) to write a short story in the style of *William's Version*. Much of the story will be dialogue, so make sure that it is set out and punctuated accurately to help the reader. A good starting point is the line from *William's Version*: "Tell me a story," said (character's name). "Tell me about ..."

Further reading

You might like to read *Nothing to be Afraid of* by Jan Mark and *The Three Little Wolves and The Big Bad Pig* by Eugene Triviaz and Helen Oxenbury for an even more bizarre reworking of the same tale.

Welsh Incident

Robert Graves

Robert Graves (1895–1985) was one of the major writers of
the twentieth century. His work includes poetry, fiction,
biography and essays. His historical novels *I, Claudius* and
Claudius The God, narrated through the imagined voice of
the Roman Emperor Claudius, have become classics and
were successfully adapted as television drama. Graves saw
himself primarily as a poet and his earliest poetry was
published while he was serving in World War I. *Welsh
Incident* is an unusual and humorous insight into the
power of an eccentric storyteller.

'BUT that was nothing to what things came out
    From the sea-caves of Criccieth yonder.'
'What were they? Mermaids? dragons? ghosts?'
'Nothing at all of any things like that.'
'What were they, then?'
                    'All sorts of queer things,
Things never seen or heard or written about,
Very strange, un-Welsh, utterly peculiar
Things. Oh, solid enough they seemed to touch,
Had anyone dared it. Marvellous creation,
All various shapes and sizes and no sizes,
All new, each perfectly unlike his neighbour,
Though all came moving slowly out together.'
'Describe just one of them.'
                    'I am unable.'

'What were their colours?'
               'Mostly nameless colours,
Colours you'd like to see; but one was puce
Or perhaps more like crimson, but not purplish.
Some had no colour.'
             'Tell me, had they legs?'
'Not a leg or foot among them that I saw.'
'But did these things come out in any order?
What o'clock was it? What was the day of the week?
Who else was present? How was the weather?'
'I was coming to that. It was half-past three
On Easter Tuesday last. The sun was shining.
The Harlech Silver Band played *Marchog Jesu*
On thirty-seven shimmering instruments,
Collecting for Carnarvon's (Fever) Hospital Fund.
The populations of Pwllheli, Criccieth,
Portmadoc, Borth, Tremadoc, Penrhyndeudraeth,
Were all assembled. Criccieth's mayor addressed them
First in good Welsh and then in fluent English,
Twisting his fingers in his chain of office,
Welcoming the things. They came out on the sand,
Not keeping time to the band, moving seaward
Silently at a snail's pace. But at last
The most odd, indescribable thing of all
Which hardly one man there could see for wonder
Did something recognizably a something.'
'Well, what?'
             'It made a noise.'
                 'A frightening noise?'
'No, no.'
            'A musical noise? A noise of scuffling?'

'No, but a very loud, respectable noise –
Like groaning to oneself on Sunday morning
In Chapel, close before the second psalm.'
'What did the mayor do?'
                    'I was coming to that.'

Activities

Reading

1 Who do you think the Welsh witness is talking to?
2 Where do you imagine the conversation taking place?
3 How does the witness describe the incident last Easter Tuesday?

Language study

4 In the first line, the witness refers to 'things'. Collect a list of all the other nouns and noun phrases he uses to refer to the 'things'.
5 Find 'But that was nothing' and 'I was coming to that' in the poem. What is the pronoun 'that' referring to in these lines?

Speaking and listening

6 Prepare a live news commentary of the Easter Tuesday incident. Use words and phrases from the text, such as: As I speak to you from outside the caves of Criccieth.
7 Work with a partner to invent a recount of your own local 'incident'. A local witness is being interviewed by a visitor to the area. First, prepare a list of questions. Then prepare words and phrases for the witness to use so that they give away no hard information. Present or record your dialogue.

Writing

8 Write the headline and first sentence of a news report of this incident in a national newspaper. (Note: the first sentence of a news story usually tells the reader who/what/where/when the incident took place, and is written in the past tense.)
9 Use the Speaking and listening task (above) as the basis for a written dialogue between two characters. One asks the questions; the other gives vague answers. Set out and punctuate the speech appropriately. You might use 'But that was nothing compared to ...'

from *A Kestrel for a Knave*

Barry Hines

Barry Hines was born in a mining village near Barnsley in 1939. After leaving school, he worked as an apprentice mining surveyor and then as a teacher before becoming a writer. His most well-known novel, *A Kestrel for a Knave*, written in 1968, draws on Hines's experiences as a child and then as a teacher in Barnsley. It was later made into the film *Kes*.

This incident is set in an English lesson in a secondary school.

H E swung one arm and indicated the board behind him. On it was printed:

FACT AND FICTION

"What did we say fact was, Armitage?"

"Something that's happened, Sir."

"Right. Something that has happened. Something that we know is real. The things that we read about in newspapers, or hear on the news. Events, accidents, meetings; the things that we see with our own eyes, the things all about us; all these are facts. Have you got that? Is that clear?"

Chorus: "Yes, Sir."

"Right then. Now if I asked Anderson for some facts about himself, what could he tell us?"

"Sir! Sir!"

"All right! All right! Just put your hands up. There's no need to jump down my throat. Jordan?"

"He's wearing jeans."

"Good. Mitchell?"

"He's got black hair."

"Yes. Fisher?"

"He lives down Shallowbank Crescent."

"Do you, Anderson?"

"Yes, Sir."

"Right then. Now all these are facts about Anderson, but they're not particularly interesting facts. Perhaps Anderson can tell us something about himself that *is* interesting. A really interesting fact."

There was a massive "Woooo!" from the rest of the class. Mr Farthing grinned and rode it; then he raised his hands to control it.

"Quietly now. Quietly."

The class quietened, still grinning. Anderson stared at his desk, blushing.

"I don't know owt, Sir."

"Anything at all Anderson, anything that's happened to you, or that you've seen which sticks in your mind."

"I can't think of owt, Sir."

"What about when you were little? Everybody remembers something about when they were little. It doesn't have to be fantastic, just something that you've remembered."

Anderson began to smile and looked up.

"There's summat. It's nowt though."

"It must be if you remember it."

"It's daft really."

"Well tell us then, and let's all have a laugh."

"Well it was once when I was a kid. I was at Junior

school, I think, or somewhere like that, and went down to
Fowlers Pond, me and this other kid. Reggie Clay they
called him, he didn't come to this school; he flitted and
went away somewhere. Anyway it was Spring, tadpole time,
and it's swarming with tadpoles down there in Spring.
Edges of t'pond are all black with 'em, and me and this
other kid started to catch 'em. It was easy, all you did, you
just put your hands together and scooped a handful of
water up and you'd got a handful of tadpoles. Anyway we
were mucking about with 'em, picking 'em up and chucking
'em back and things, and we were on about taking some
home, but we'd no jam jars. So this kid, Reggie, says, 'Take
thi wellingtons off and put some in there, they'll be all right
'til tha gets home.' So I took 'em off and we put some water
in 'em and then we started to put taddies in 'em. We kept
ladling 'em in and I says to this kid, 'Let's have a
competition, thee have one welli' and I'll have t'other, and
we'll see who can get most in!' So he started to fill one welli'
and I started to fill t'other. We must have been at it hours,
and they got thicker and thicker, until at t'end there was no
water left in 'em, they were just jam packed wi'taddies.

"You ought to have seen 'em, all black and shiny, right up
to t'top. When we'd finished we kept dipping us fingers into
'em and whipping 'em up at each other, all shouting and
excited like. Then this kid says to me, 'I bet tha daren't put
one on.' And I says, 'I bet tha daren't.' So we said we'd put
one on each. We wouldn't though, we kept reckoning to,
then running away, so we tossed up and him who lost had
to do it first. And I lost, oh, and you'd to take your socks off
an' all. So I took my socks off, and kept looking at this welli'
full of taddies, and this kid kept saying, 'Go on then, tha

frightened, tha frightened.' I was an' all. Anyway I shut my eyes and started to put my foot in. Oooo. It was just like putting your feet into live jelly. They were frozen. And when my foot went down, they all came over t'top of my wellington, and when I got my foot to t'bottom, I could feel 'em all squashing about between my toes.

"Anyway, I'd done it, and I says to this kid, 'Thee put thine on now.' But he wouldn't, he was dead scared, so I put it on instead. I'd got used to it then, it was all right after a bit; it sent your legs all excited and tingling like. When I'd got 'em both on I started to walk up to this kid, waving my arms and making spook noises; and as I walked they all came squelching over t'tops again and ran down t'sides. This kid looked frightened to death, he kept looking down at my wellies so I tried to run at him and they all spurted up my legs. You ought to have seen him. He just screamed out and ran home roaring.

"It was a funny feeling though when he'd gone; all quiet, with nobody there, and up to t'knees in tadpoles."

Silence. The class up to their knees in tadpoles.

Activities

Reading
1 At first Anderson does not want to tell the story. Why?
2 Anderson's account is full of minor details (for example, the name of the pond and where Reggie Clay went to school). What is the effect of all this detail?
3 What does the writer mean by describing the class as 'up to their knees in tadpoles' in the last line?

Speaking and listening
4 Do you know of anyone you think is a skilful storyteller? What are the skills and qualities that a storyteller should have?

Language study
5 *A Kestrel for a Knave* is set in Barnsley and the characters speak in local dialect. Make a list of local words used and give the standard English equivalent. For example: owt (local)/anything (standard English). How important do you think the use of dialect is to the story's effect? Give reasons for your answer.

Writing
6 Anderson's story begins, 'it was once when I was a kid'. He quickly establishes the setting and characters and moves onto the main events. Write the opening paragraph of your own personal story. Include details that help the reader to picture the scene (for example, the weather and the time of day).
7 Write Mr Farthing's assessment record of Anderson's talk. You could comment on his confidence, range of vocabulary, use of humour and skill in engaging the listeners.

Further reading

You may also like to read in full *A Kestrel for a Knave* by Barry Hines or see *Kes*, the video film of the book.

I Shot the Sheriff

Bob Marley

Born in Jamaica in 1945, the singer-songwriter Bob Marley rose from humble beginnings to become a global superstar. He was the leading pioneer of reggae music, and many of his songs became anthems of liberation for people all over the world. When he died in 1981, his funeral in Jamaica was like that of a king.

I Shot the Sheriff, recorded in 1973, is both a plea for justice and a cry of defiance on behalf of the oppressed.

I shot the sheriff, but I didn't shoot no deputy
I shot the sheriff, but I didn't shoot no deputy

All around in my hometown
They're tryin' to track me down, yeah
They say they want to bring me in guilty
For the killing of a deputy, for the life of a deputy
But I say

Oh, I shot the sheriff, but I swear it was in self defence
I said, I shot the sheriff, Oh Lord
And they say it is a capital offence
Hear this

Sheriff John Brown always hated me
For what I don't know

Ev'ry time I plant a seed
He said, "Kill it before it grows."
He said, "Kill them before they grow."

And so,
Read it in the news

I shot the sheriff, but I swear it was in self defence
Where was the deputy?
I said I shot the sheriff but I swear it was in self defence

Freedom came my way one day
And I started out of town, yeah!
All of a sudden I saw Sheriff John Brown
Aiming to shoot me down
So I shot, I shot, I shot him down
And I say, if I am guilty I will pay

I shot the sheriff, but I say, but I didn't shoot no deputy
I shot the sheriff, but I didn't shoot no deputy

Reflexes had the better of me
And what is to be must be
Ev'ry day the bucket a-go-a well
One day the bottom a-go drop out
One day the bottom a-go drop out
I say I shot the sheriff, but I didn't shoot the deputy, no.

Activities

Reading
1 What is the singer's attitude to the crime?
2 Why do you think this song became popular as an anthem for the oppressed? Can you think of any recent songs that also make a plea for justice?

Language study
'Ev'ry day the bucket a-go-a well
One day the bottom a-go drop out.'
3 Explain this metaphor.

Speaking and listening
4 Songs have always been a popular way of telling stories: from traditional ballads through to current day hip-hop. Draw up a track listing for a CD of story songs.

Compare and contrast
5 Read *An Arrest* by Ambrose Bierce (page 97), another outlaw story. What similarities do you notice between the main characters in the song and the story? Which character do you feel most sorry for? Why?

Further listening

You may like to listen to the song on *One Love: The Bob Marley Story* by Island Records.

Other examples of songs telling stories include *I Fought the Law* by The Bobby Fuller Four or by The Clash, and *Levi Stubbs' Tears* by Billy Bragg and *Stan* by Eminem.

The Shah of Blah

Salman Rushdie

Salman Rushdie was born in Bombay, India, in 1947 and studied in England. After working in the theatre and advertising, he turned to writing novels and won the Booker Prize for his second book, *Midnight's Children*.

Haroun and the Sea of Stories is Rushdie's first book for children. This book has many of the features of Rushdie's adult novels: brilliant wordplay, a sharp sense of humour, elements of Indian culture and a man of many stories.

THERE was once, in the country of Alifbay, a sad city, the saddest of cities, a city so ruinously sad that it had forgotten its name. It stood by a mournful sea full of glumfish, which were so miserable to eat that they made people belch with melancholy even though the skies were blue.

In the north of the sad city stood mighty factories in which (so I'm told) sadness was actually manufactured, packaged and sent all over the world, which never seemed to get enough of it. Black smoke poured out of the chimneys of the sadness factories and hung over the city like bad news.

And in the depths of the city, beyond an old zone of ruined buildings that looked like broken hearts, there lived a happy young fellow by the name of Haroun, the only child of the storyteller Rashid Khalifa, whose cheerfulness was famous throughout that unhappy metropolis,[1] and

---

[1] *metropolis:* city

whose never-ending stream of tall, short and winding tales had earned him not one but two nicknames. To his admirers he was Rashid the Ocean of Notions, as stuffed with cheery stories as the sea was full of glumfish; but to his jealous rivals he was the Shah of Blah. To his wife, Soraya, Rashid was for many years as loving a husband as anyone could wish for, and during these years Haroun grew up in a home in which, instead of misery and frowns, he had his father's ready laughter and his mother's sweet voice raised in song.

Then something went wrong. (Maybe the sadness of the city finally crept in through their windows.)

The day Soraya stopped singing, in the middle of a line, as if someone had thrown a switch, Haroun guessed there was trouble brewing. But he never suspected how much.

Rashid Khalifa was so busy making up and telling stories that he didn't notice that Soraya no longer sang; which probably made things worse. But then Rashid was a busy man, in constant demand, he was the Ocean of Notions, the famous Shah of Blah. And what with all his rehearsals and performances, Rashid was so often on stage that he lost track of what was going on in his own home. He sped around the city and the country telling stories, while Soraya stayed home, turning cloudy and even a little thunderous and brewing up quite a storm.

Haroun went with his father whenever he could, because the man was a magician, it couldn't be denied. He would climb up on to some little makeshift stage in a dead-end alley packed with raggedy children and toothless old-timers, all squatting in the dust; and once he got going even the city's many wandering cows would stop and cock their ears, and monkeys would jabber approvingly from rooftops and the parrots in the trees would imitate his voice.

Haroun often thought of his father as a Juggler, because his stories were really lots of different tales juggled together, and Rashid kept them going in a sort of dizzy whirl, and never made a mistake.

Where did all these stories come from? It seemed that all Rashid had to do was to part his lips in a plump red smile and out would pop some brand-new saga,[2] complete with sorcery, love-interest, princesses, wicked uncles, fat aunts, mustachioed gangsters in yellow check pants, fantastic locations, cowards, heroes, fights, and half a dozen catchy, hummable tunes. "Everything comes from somewhere," Haroun reasoned, "so these stories can't simply come out of thin air ...?"

But whenever he asked his father this most important of questions, the Shah of Blah would narrow his (to tell the truth) slightly bulging eyes, and pat his wobbly stomach, and stick his thumb between his lips while he made ridiculous drinking noises, *glug glug glug,* Haroun hated it when his father acted this way. "No, come on, where do they come from really?" he'd insist, and Rashid would wiggle his eyebrows mysteriously and make witchy fingers in the air.

"From the great Story Sea," he'd reply. "I drink the warm Story Waters and then I feel full of steam."

Haroun found this statement intensely irritating. "Where do you keep this hot water, then?" he argued craftily. "In hot-water bottles, I suppose. Well, I've never seen any."

---

[2] **saga:** tale

"It comes out of an invisible Tap installed by one of the Water Genies," said Rashid with a straight face. "You have to be a subscriber."

"And how do you become a subscriber?"

"Oh," said the Shah of Blah, "that's much Too Complicated To Explain."

"Anyhow," said Haroun grumpily, "I've never see a Water Genie, either." Rashid shrugged. "You're never up in time to see the milkman," he pointed out, "but you don't mind drinking the milk. So now kindly desist from this Iffing and Butting and be happy with the stories you enjoy." And that was the end of that.

Except that one day Haroun asked one question too many, and then all hell broke loose.

Activities

Reading

1 How does Salman Rushdie set the scene and the mood in the opening two paragraphs?
2 What were the two nicknames for Rashid Kalifa?
3 We are told that Rashid had rivals. Who might these rivals be?
4 Rashid is described as a lively and energetic man. Find words and phrases that are used to give that impression.
5 Why does Rashid not tell his son where the stories come from?

Language study

6 In the first sentence, Salman Rushdie uses longer and longer noun phrases to describe the city, for example, 'a sad city, the saddest of cities, a city so ruinously sad that it had forgotten its name.' What is the effect of these phrases?
7 Try the same effect starting with a simple phrase, beginning with, perhaps, 'an angry man', or 'a fast car', or 'a noisy classroom'.

Speaking and listening

8 Rashid's stories come complete with 'sorcery, love-interest, princesses, wicked uncles, fat aunts, mustachioed gangsters in yellow check pants ...' What do you think are the vital ingredients of a good tale?

Writing

9 Read the two short paragraphs at the top of page 55 starting, 'Then something went wrong.' Notice how they hint at trouble without giving anything anyway. Write a short paragraph that hints at future trouble in a story.
10 Write a description of a colourful character for a story. Use dialogue, action and other characters' reactions to support your description.

Further reading

You may also like to read in full *Haroun and the Sea of Stories* by Salman Rushdie.

Lies

"Any fool can tell the truth, but it requires a man of some
sense to know how to lie well."

Samuel Butler

"A mixture of a lie doth ever add pleasure."

Francis Bacon, *Essays: of Truth*

The Open Window

Saki

Saki was the writing name of Hector Hugh Munro (1870–1916). He started his career as a police officer in Burma before moving to London to write political satire for a newspaper. His first short stories were published in 1904 and over the next 10 years he wrote the stories for which he is now best known. He enlisted as a trooper in World War I and was killed in action, shot in the head, in 1916.

His stories are both funny and sinister, and often show children or even animals exacting cruel revenge on the adults around them. *The Open Window* is a fine example of this.

"My aunt will be down presently, Mr Nuttel," said a very self-possessed[1] young lady of fifteen; "in the meantime you must try and put up with me."

Framton Nuttel endeavoured to say the correct something which should duly flatter the niece of the moment without unduly discounting the aunt that was to come. Privately he doubted more than ever whether these formal visits on a succession of total strangers would do much towards helping the nerve cure which he was supposed to be undergoing.

"I know how it will be," his sister had said when he was preparing to migrate to this rural retreat; "you will bury

---

[1] *self-possessed:* calm

yourself down there and not speak to a living soul, and your nerves will be worse than ever from moping. I shall just give you letters of introduction to all the people I know there. Some of them, as far as I can remember, were quite nice."

Framton wondered whether Mrs Sappleton, the lady to whom he was presenting one of the letters of introduction, came into the nice division.

"Do you know many of the people round here?" asked the niece, when she judged that they had had sufficient silent communion.[2]

"Hardly a soul," said Framton. "My sister was staying here, at the rectory, you know, some four years ago, and she gave me letters of introduction to some of the people here."

He made the last statement in a tone of distinct regret.

"Then you know practically nothing about my aunt?" pursued the self-possessed young lady.

"Only her name and address," admitted the caller. He was wondering whether Mrs Sappleton was in the married or widowed state. An undefinable something about the room seemed to suggest masculine habitation.

"Her great tragedy happened just three years ago," said the child; "that would be since your sister's time."

"Her tragedy?" asked Framton; somehow in this restful country spot tragedies seemed out of place.

"You may wonder why we keep that window wide open on an October afternoon," said the niece, indicating a large French window that opened on to a lawn.

---

[2] *silent communion:* sitting together in silence

"It is quite warm for that time of year," said Framton; "but has that window got anything to do with the tragedy?"

"Out through that window, three years ago to a day, her husband and her two young brothers went off for their day's shooting. They never came back. In crossing the moor to their favourite snipe-shooting ground they were all three engulfed in a treacherous piece of bog. It had been that dreadful wet summer, you know, and places that were safe in other years gave way suddenly without warning. Their bodies were never recovered. That was the dreadful part of it." Here the child's voice lost its self-possessed note and became falteringly human. "Poor aunt always thinks that they will come back some day, they and the little brown spaniel that was lost with them, and walk in that window just as they used to do. That is why the window is kept open every evening till it is quite dusk. Poor dear aunt, she has often told me how they went out, her husband with his white waterproof coat over his arm, and Ronnie, her youngest brother, singing, 'Bertie, why do you bound?' as he always did to tease her, because she said that it got on her nerves. Do you know, sometimes on still, quiet evenings like this, I almost get a creepy feeling that they will all walk in through that window – "

She broke off with a little shudder. It was a relief to Framton when the aunt bustled into the room with a whirl of apologies for being late in making her appearance.

"I hope Vera has been amusing you?" she said.

"She has been very interesting," said Framton.

"I hope you don't mind the window open," said Mrs Sappleton briskly; "my husband and brothers will be home directly from shooting, and they always come in this way.

They've been out for snipe in the marshes today, so they'll make a fine mess over my poor carpets. So like you men-folk, isn't it?"

She rattled on cheerfully about the shooting and the scarcity of birds, and the prospects for duck in the winter. To Framton it was all purely horrible. He made a desperate but only partially successful effort to turn the talk on to a less ghastly topic; he was conscious that his hostess was giving him only a fragment of her attention, and her eyes were constantly straying past him to the open window and the lawn beyond. It was certainly an unfortunate coincidence that he should have paid his visit on this tragic anniversary.

"The doctors agree in ordering me complete rest, an absence of mental excitement, and avoidance of anything in the nature of violent physical exercise," announced Framton, who laboured under the tolerably widespread delusion that total strangers and chance acquaintances are hungry for the least detail of one's ailments and infirmities,[3] their cause and cure. "On the matter of diet they are not so much in agreement," he continued.

"No?" said Mrs Sappleton, in a voice which only replaced a yawn at the last moment. Then she suddenly brightened into alert attention – but not to what Framton was saying.

"Here they are at last!" she cried. "Just in time for tea, and don't they look as if they were muddy up to the eyes!"

Framton shivered slightly and turned towards the niece with a look intended to convey sympathetic comprehension. The child was staring out through the open

---

[3] *infirmities:* illnesses

window with dazed horror in her eyes. In a chill shock of nameless fear Framton swung round in his seat and looked in the same direction.

In the deepening twilight three figures were walking across the lawn towards the window; they all carried guns under their arms, and one of them was additionally burdened with a white coat hung over his shoulders. A tired brown spaniel kept close at their heels. Noiselessly they neared the house, and then a hoarse young voice chanted out of the dusk: "I said, Bertie, why do you bound?"

Framton grabbed wildly at his stick and hat; the hall-door, the gravel-drive, and the front gate were dimly noted stages in his headlong retreat. A cyclist coming along the road had to run into the hedge to avoid imminent collision.

"Here we are, my dear," said the bearer of the white mackintosh, coming in through the window; "fairly muddy, but most of it's dry. Who was that who bolted out as we came up?"

"A most extraordinary man, a Mr Nuttel," said Mrs Sappleton; "could only talk about his illnesses, and dashed off without a word of good-bye or apology when you arrived. One would think he had seen a ghost."

"I expect it was the spaniel," said the niece calmly; "he told me he had a horror of dogs. He was once hunted into a cemetery somewhere on the banks of the Ganges by a pack of pariah dogs,[4] and had to spend the night in a newly dug grave with the creatures snarling and grinning and foaming just above him. Enough to make any one lose their nerve."

Romance at short notice was her speciality.

---

[4] **pariah dogs:** half-wild dogs

Activities

Reading
1 What was the purpose of Framton Nuttel's visit to the country house?
2 What is Mrs Stapleton's opinion of Nuttel?
3 Apart from what she says, what else does the girl do to convince Nuttel?
4 At what point can we tell for certain that the girl has been lying?

Language study
5 'Romance at short notice was her speciality' is a euphemism for (a polite and formal way of saying) 'she was a very good liar'. Make up euphemisms for 'he is very violent', 'she is rude', and other insults.

Speaking and listening
6 If the main character had been an adult instead of a young girl, would the story work differently?
7 Work in threes. Prepare three anecdotes to tell a larger group: one should be true and the others false. Your listeners will have to decide which story is the true one. Important features to include in your account are:
   ● the setting (when/where)
   ● the people involved (not too many characters or it becomes hard to follow)
   ● the order in which you recount the main events
   ● what you were thinking and feeling as the events happened.

Writing
8 Write a letter from Framton Nuttell to his sister giving an account of his stay in the country.
9 Write a brief explanation of how Saki makes the girl's lie seem plausible. Refer to the text to support your answer.

Compare and contrast
10 Read the extract from Anne Fine's *The Tulip Touch* (page 69), written nearly a hundred years later. Compare the way the two pieces deal with a similar theme – that of a young girl who lies expertly to adults.

Further reading

You might like to read *The Best of Saki* by Saki and *The Complete Short Stories of Saki*.

from *This Lime Tree Bower*

Conor McPherson

Born in Dublin in 1971, Conor McPherson is the youngest writer to be included in this anthology. After a string of successful theatre plays, including *The Weir*, he is now writing and directing films.

This Lime Tree Bower is one of his earliest plays, in which three young men tell tales from a small Irish seaside town. One of them, Joe, presents this unlikely yarn ...

I spent the evening with Fergus and Noel.

We were mates since being kids.

They called for me and we had nowhere to go.

We went down to the rocks where the shipwreck was. The tide was out and we could see most of it.

We were never allowed to swim out near it because a boy got stuck in it one time and died. But that was back in the seventies and none of us knew him.

The story was that the ship was carrying guns for the IRA[1] in 1920 or something and the captain was an English fellow who had fallen in love with a girl in the town.

And she was in the women's IRA.

---

[1] **IRA:** Irish Republican Army

And she got him to bring the guns over in the night. But she was supposed to marry some farmer further up the coast. And he had found out and he tipped off the Black and Tans.[2] So they arrested the girl in her house and captured the IRA men who were going down the beach to get the guns.

But the girl knocked over an oil lamp in the house and there was a huge fire.

This warned the captain of the boat and he scuttled it.

He was drowned and because a British soldier died in the fire the girl was hung.

That was the story the old lads in Reynolds' used to say about it.

But Frank told me the boat belonged to a fisherman called Vinty Duggan who crashed it after drinking a bottle of Powers.

It was hard to know who to believe.

The town was full of spoofers.[3]

Dad said he wouldn't get involved in the dispute because he was from Italy and it was none of his business.

He said that Irish people would rather make something up and if that's what they liked to do, then he had no problem.

When I told him he was forgetting I was Irish, he just told me to believe what I liked.

Or better still, make up my own spoof about the boat.

---

[2] **Black and Tans:** British Army Forces
[3] **spoofers:** people who tell joky stories

Activities

Reading
1 Which version of the shipwreck do you believe? Why?
2 Why might 'the old lads in Reynolds' pass on the tale of the IRA and the shipwreck?
3 What does Joe's Italian father think of the Irish?

Speaking and listening
4 Are there any 'spoofs' or myths that have grown up around any places in your area? Discuss any you know of. Prepare and tell a myth about a local landmark.

Language study
5 This speech uses a number of short sentences. What effect does that have on:
● the way it sounds when it is spoken aloud?
● the way the story works?

Writing
6 'He just told me to believe what I liked. Or better still, make up my own spoof about the boat.' Make up your own spoof about the boat in the bay.
7 Write an article about the bay for a tourist guidebook. Address the reader in the style of that kind of book.

from *The Tulip Touch*

Anne Fine

Anne Fine wrote her first book for children soon after having her first baby, when she was trapped in a cold flat with no access to a library. Since then she has published over 40 books for children, teenagers and adults. Her books for young adults include *The Tulip Touch*, *Goggle-Eyes*, *Flour Babies* and *Madame Doubtfire*, which was adapted into a successful film starring Robin Williams.

The Tulip Touch tells the story of a sinister young girl who lies compulsively.

SHE had no other friends. Nobody else could stand the embarrassment of pretending that they believed her awful lies.

"The army's borrowing one of our fields today. When I get home, they're going to let me drive a tank."

"Oh, I really believe that, Tulip!"

"So likely!"

They'd walk off, scoffing. I'd stare at the ground, and, guess what, I'd feel *sorry* for her. I knew she was making a fool of me in front of everyone. (Only an idiot would make a show of believing her rubbish.) But instead of just walking away, exasperated,[1] like everyone else, I'd try taking her arm and distracting her.

"Want to play *Road of Bones* on the way home?"

---

[1] *exasperated:* annoyed

She'd shake me off, rude and ungrateful. Even back then I had to ask myself why I stayed around. It wasn't out of pity, I knew that. Nobody *has* to carry on telling ridiculous lies, even after it's obvious that no one believes them.

"I've won a big competition. I found a scratchcard in my cornflakes and I was lucky. So now I've won this beautiful yellow silk dress."

Next time we bought sweets in Harry's supermarket, I'd linger by the breakfast cereal shelves.

"There's nothing about a competition on any of these packets."

"No. It was a scratchcard inside."

"Strange that no one else got one."

"They only sent out a few as a special anniversary thing. That's why the prize is a yellow silk dress. It's the very same one that the model wore in their first advert."

That's what Dad came to call the Tulip touch – that tiny detail that almost made you wonder if she might, just for once, be telling the truth.

"And then this man went grey and keeled over. And as I was phoning for the ambulance, his fingers kept twitching, and his wedding ring made a tiny little pinging noise against the metal of the drain."

"So I wasn't at school because the police needed one extra person my age and size, for a line-up. They wouldn't say why they'd arrested the girl, but one of them did tell me that he thought she was Polish."

"Ah!" Dad would murmur in unfeigned[2] admiration. "Polish? The perfect Tulip touch!"

---

[2] *unfeigned:* real

She'd give him a pained wooden stare. "Sorry?"

"Nothing."

He'd turn away, of course, to hide his grin. But I'd be left to see the look of venom on her face. Tulip loathed being teased. It was as if the moment these stupid stories were out of her mouth, she believed them completely, and anyone who queried even a tiny part of them was going to be her enemy, and hated for ever.

So it was Dad, not me, who risked a bit of mischief a couple of weeks later.

"So where's the great yellow dress, Tulip? How come you haven't brought it round to show us yet?"

She looked surprised. "Didn't I tell you? I had it ready in a bag. Then Mum knocked over a bottle of bleach, and some got on the sleeve. So she's posted it off to a big firm in Chichester that does a lot of mending for the royal family, to see if they can patch it from the hem."

Dad watched her, spellbound.

Activities

Reading
1 What does the dad mean by 'the Tulip touch'? Give three examples from the extract.
2 The girl narrator admits that she is Tulip's only friend. Why do you think she sticks by her?
3 What is the attitude of the girl's father to Tulip?

Language study
4 The narrator moves between the present and the past tense in this extract. Identify where the present tense is used. What is the effect of using the present tense in her account?
5 'She'd shake me off' (page 70) is one example of where the narrator adopts the past tense by using an auxiliary verb ('would', shortened here to 'She'd') together with a participle ('shake'). Try and find other examples of where this form is used, and write each out in full with the correct form of the auxiliary verb.
6 What can you deduce about when the narrator must be telling this story from the differences in tenses and from phrases like 'Next time ... A couple of weeks later ...'?

Speaking and listening
7 'The key to a good lie is the unnecessary detail in it.' What do you think? Discuss whether you agree or disagree.
8 As a class, set up a TV discussion show role play where the host interviews members of the public in front of a studio audience who can also make their points and challenge the guests. The title of today's show is: My Friend is a Compulsive Liar.

Writing
9 Write a letter from Natalie (the girl narrator) to a teenage magazine's problem page. She wants to explain about the lying and to ask for advice about how to handle the friendship. Write the magazine's advice in reply.
10 Write an excuse note using an elaborate lie, such as for being late for school, for failing to complete homework or for losing something you have borrowed. Include plenty of detail in the lie.

Further reading

You might like to read in full *The Tulip Touch* and *A Pack Of Liars*, both by Anne Fine.

Suspense

"I could a tale unfold whose lightest word
Would harrow up thy soul, freeze thy young blood,
Make thy two eyes, like stars, start from their spheres,
Thy knotted and combined locks to stand on end,
Like quills upon the fretful porpentine:
But this eternal blazon must not be
To ears of flesh and blood."

William Shakespeare, *Hamlet*

The Monkey's Paw

W.W. Jacobs

W.W. Jacobs (1863–1943) was born in Wapping, London. He became a clerk in the Civil Service before he began publishing his short stories, many of which recount the escapades of roguish characters. However, by far his most famous work is this classic tale of the macabre ...

I

WITHOUT, the night was cold and wet, but in the small parlour[1] of Laburnam Villa the blinds were drawn and the fire burned brightly. Father and son were at chess, the former, who possessed ideas about the game involving radical changes, putting his king into such sharp and unnecessary perils that it even provoked comment from the white-haired old lady knitting placidly by the fire.

"Hark at the wind," said Mr White, who, having seen a fatal mistake after it was too late, was amiably desirous of preventing his son from seeing it.

"I'm listening," said the latter, grimly surveying the board as he stretched out his hand. "Check."

"I should hardly think that he'd come tonight," said his father, with his hand poised over the board.

"Mate," replied the son.

"That's the worst of living so far out," bawled Mr White,

---

[1] *parlour:* sitting room

with sudden and unlooked-for violence; "of all the beastly, slushy, out-of-the-way places to live in, this is the worst. Pathway's a bog, and the road's a torrent. I don't know what people are thinking about. I suppose because only two houses on the road are let, they think it doesn't matter."

"Never mind, dear," said his wife soothingly; "perhaps you'll win the next one."

Mr White looked up sharply, just in time to intercept a knowing glance between mother and son. The words died away on his lips, and he hid a guilty grin in his thin grey beard.

"There he is," said Herbert White, as the gate banged to loudly and heavy footsteps came toward the door.

The old man rose with hospitable haste, and opening the door, was heard condoling with the new arrival. The new arrival also condoled with himself, so that Mrs White said, "Tut, tut!" and coughed gently as her husband entered the room, followed by a tall burly man, beady of eye and rubicund[2] of visage.

"Sergeant-Major Morris," he said, introducing him.

The sergeant-major shook hands, and taking the proffered seat by the fire, watched contentedly while his host got out whisky and tumblers and stood a small copper kettle on the fire.

At the third glass his eyes got brighter, and he began to talk, the little family circle regarding with eager interest this visitor from distant parts, as he squared his broad shoulders in the chair and spoke of strange scenes and doughty deeds;[3] of wars and plagues and strange peoples.

---

[2] **rubicund:** red
[3] **doughty deeds:** brave actions

"Twenty-one years of it," said Mr White, nodding at his wife and son. "When he went away he was a slip of a youth in the warehouse. Now look at him."

"He don't look to have taken much harm," said Mrs White, politely.

"I'd like to go to India myself," said the old man, "just to look round a bit, you know."

"Better where you are," said the sergeant-major, shaking his head. He put down the empty glass, and sighing softly, shook it again.

"I should like to see those old temples and fakirs[4] and jugglers," said the old man. "What was that you started telling me the other day about a monkey's paw or something, Morris?"

"Nothing," said the soldier hastily. "Leastways, nothing worth hearing."

"Monkey's paw?" said Mrs White curiously.

"Well, it's just a bit of what you might call magic, perhaps," said the sergeant-major off-handedly.

His three listeners leaned forward eagerly. The visitor absentmindedly put his empty glass to his lips and then set it down again. His host filled it for him.

"To look at," said the sergeant-major, fumbling in his pocket, "it's just an ordinary little paw, dried to a mummy."

He took something out of his pocket and proffered it. Mrs White drew back with a grimace, but her son, taking it, examined it curiously.

"And what is there special about it?" inquired Mr White, as he took it from his son and, having examined it, placed it upon the table.

---

[4] *fakirs:* wandering religious beggars

"It had a spell put on it by an old fakir," said the sergeant-major, "a very holy man. He wanted to show that fate ruled people's lives, and that those who interfered with it did so to their sorrow. He put a spell on it so that three separate men could each have three wishes from it."

His manner was so impressive that his hearers were conscious that their light laughter jarred somewhat.

"Well, why don't you have three, sir?" said Herbert White cleverly.

The soldier regarded him in the way that middle age is wont to regard presumptuous[5] youth. "I have," he said quietly, and his blotchy face whitened.

"And did you really have the three wishes granted?" asked Mrs White.

"I did," said the sergeant-major, and his glass tapped against his strong teeth.

"And has anybody else wished?" inquired the old lady.

"The first man had his three wishes, yes," was the reply. "I don't know what the first two were, but the third was for death. That's how I got the paw."

His tones were so grave that a hush fell upon the group.

"If you've had your three wishes, it's no good to you now, then, Morris," said the old man at last. "What do you keep it for?"

The soldier shook his head. "Fancy, I suppose," he said slowly.

"If you could have another three wishes," said the old man, eyeing him keenly, "would you have them?"

"I don't know," said the other. "I don't know."

---

[5] **presumptious:** cheeky

He took the paw, and dangling it between his front finger and thumb, suddenly threw it upon the fire. White, with a slight cry, stooped down and snatched it off.

"Better let it burn," said the soldier solemnly.

"If you don't want it, Morris," said the old man, "give it to me."

"I won't," said his friend doggedly. "I threw it on the fire. If you keep it, don't blame me for what happens. Pitch it on the fire again, like a sensible man."

The other shook his head and examined his new possession closely. "How do you do it?" he inquired.

"Hold it up in your right hand and wish aloud," said the sergeant-major, "but I warn you of the consequences."

"Sounds like the *Arabian Nights*," said Mrs White, as she rose and began to set the supper. "Don't you think you might wish for four pairs of hands for me?"

Her husband drew the talisman[6] from his pocket and then all three burst into laughter as the sergeant-major, with a look of alarm on his face, caught him by the arm.

"If you must wish," he said gruffly, "wish for something sensible."

Mr White dropped it back into his pocket and, placing chairs, motioned his friend to the table. In the business of supper the talisman was partly forgotten, and afterward the three sat listening in an enthralled fashion to a second instalment of the soldier's adventures in India.

"If the tale about the monkey paw is not more truthful than those he has been telling us," said Herbert, as the door closed behind their guest, just in time for him to catch the last train, "we shan't make much out of it."

---

[6] **talisman:** lucky charm

"Did you give him anything for it, father?" inquired Mrs White, regarding her husband closely.

"A trifle," said he, colouring slightly. "He didn't want it, but I made him take it. And he pressed me again to throw it away."

"Likely," said Herbert, with pretended horror. "Why, we're going to be rich, and famous, and happy. Wish to be an emperor, father, to begin with; then you can't be henpecked."

He darted round the table, pursued by the maligned Mrs White armed with an antimacassar.[7]

Mr White took the paw from his pocket and eyed it dubiously. "I don't know what to wish for, and that's a fact," he said slowly. "It seems to me I've got all I want."

"If you only cleared the house, you'd be quite happy, wouldn't you?" said Herbert, with his hand on his shoulder. "Well, wish for two hundred pounds, then; that'll just do it."

His father, smiling shamefacedly at his own credulity, held up the talisman, as his son, with a solemn face somewhat marred by a wink at his mother, sat down at the piano and struck a few impressive chords.

"I wish for two hundred pounds," said the old man distinctly.

A fine crash from the piano greeted the words, interrupted by a shuddering cry from the old man. His wife and son ran toward him.

"It moved," he cried, with a glance of disgust at the object as it lay on the floor. "As I wished it twisted in my hands like a snake."

"Well, I don't see the money," said his son, as he picked it up and placed it on the table, "and I bet I never shall."

---

[7] **antimacassar:** a cloth used to protect the arms and back of chairs

"It must have been your fancy, father," said his wife, regarding him anxiously.

He shook his head. "Never mind, though; there's no harm done, but it gave me a shock all the same."

They sat down by the fire again while the two men finished their pipes. Outside, the wind was higher than ever, and the old man started nervously at the sound of a door banging upstairs. A silence unusual and depressing settled upon all three, which lasted until the old couple rose to retire for the night.

"I expect you'll find the cash tied up in a big bag in the middle of your bed," said Herbert, as he bade them goodnight, "and something horrible squatting up on top of the wardrobe watching you as you pocket your ill-gotten gains."

He sat alone in the darkness, gazing at the dying fire, and seeing faces in it. The last face was so horrible and so simian[8] that he gazed at it in amazement. It got so vivid that, with a little uneasy laugh, he felt on the table for a glass containing a little water to throw over it. His hand grasped the monkey's paw, and with a little shiver he wiped his hand on his coat and went up to bed.

II

In the brightness of the wintry sun next morning as it streamed over the breakfast table Herbert laughed at his fears. There was an air of prosaic wholesomeness about the room which it had lacked on the previous night, and the dirty, shrivelled little paw was pitched on the sideboard

---

[8] **simian:** monkey-like

with a carelessness which betokened no great belief in its virtues.

"I suppose all old soldiers are the same," said Mrs White. "The idea of our listening to such nonsense! How could wishes be granted in these days? And if they could, how could two hundred pounds hurt you, father?"

"Might drop on his head from the sky," said the frivolous Herbert.

"Morris said the things happened so naturally," said his father, "that you might if you so wished attribute it to coincidence."

"Well, don't break into the money before I come back," said Herbert, as he rose from the table. "I'm afraid it'll turn you into a mean, avaricious[9] man, and we shall have to disown you."

His mother laughed, and following him to the door, watched him down the road, and returning to the breakfast table, was very happy at the expense of her husband's credulity. All of which did not prevent her from scurrying to the door at the postman's knock, nor prevent her from referring somewhat shortly to retired sergeant-majors of bibulous[10] habits when she found that the post brought a tailor's bill.

"Herbert will have some more of his funny remarks, I expect, when he comes home," she said, as they sat at dinner.

"I dare say," said Mr White, pouring himself out some beer; "but for all that, the thing moved in my hand; that I'll swear to."

---

[9] *avaricious:* greedy
[10] *bibulous:* alcoholic

"You thought it did," said the old lady soothingly.

"I say it did," replied the other. "There was no thought about it; I had just – What's the matter?"

His wife made no reply. She was watching the mysterious movements of a man outside, who, peering in an undecided fashion at the house, appeared to be trying to make up his mind to enter. In mental connection with the two hundred pounds, she noticed that the stranger was well dressed and wore a silk hat of glossy newness. Three times he paused at the gate, and then walked on again. The fourth time he stood with his hand upon it, and then with sudden resolution flung it open and walked up the path. Mrs White at the same moment placed her hands behind her, and hurriedly unfastening the strings of her apron, put that useful article of apparel beneath the cushion of her chair.

She brought the stranger, who seemed ill at ease, into the room. He gazed at her furtively, and listened in a preoccupied fashion as the old lady apologized for the appearance of the room, and her husband's coat, a garment which he usually reserved for the garden. She then waited as patiently as her sex would permit, for him to broach[11] his business, but he was at first strangely silent.

"I – was asked to call," he said at last, and stooped and picked a piece of cotton from his trousers. "I come from Maw and Meggins."

The old lady started. "Is anything the matter?" she asked breathlessly. "Has anything happened to Herbert? What is it? What is it?"

---

[11] **broach:** talk about

Her husband interposed. "There, there, mother," he said hastily. "Sit down, and don't jump to conclusions. You've not brought bad news, I'm sure, sir" and he eyed the other wistfully.

"I'm sorry – " began the visitor.

"Is he hurt?" demanded the mother.

The visitor bowed in assent. "Badly hurt," he said quietly, "but he is not in any pain."

"Oh, thank God!" said the old woman, clasping her hands. "Thank God for that! Thank – "

She broke off suddenly as the sinister meaning of the assurance dawned upon her and she saw the awful confirmation of her fears in the other's averted face. She caught her breath, and turning to her slower-witted husband, laid her trembling old hand upon his. There was a long silence.

"He was caught in the machinery," said the visitor at length, in a low voice.

"Caught in the machinery," repeated Mr White, in a dazed fashion, "yes."

He sat staring blankly out at the window, and taking his wife's hand between his own, pressed it as he had been wont to do in their old courting days nearly forty years before.

"He was the only one left to us," he said, turning gently to the visitor. "It is hard."

The other coughed, and rising, walked slowly to the window. "The firm wished me to convey their sincere sympathy with you in your great loss," he said, without looking round. "I beg that you will understand I am only their servant and merely obeying orders."

There was no reply; the old woman's face was white, her eyes staring, and her breath inaudible; on the husband's face was a look such as his friend the sergeant might have carried into his first action.

"I was to say that Maw and Meggins disclaim all responsibility," continued the other. "They admit no liability at all, but in consideration of your son's services they wish to present you with a certain sum as compensation."

Mr White dropped his wife's hand, and rising to his feet, gazed with a look of horror at his visitor. His dry lips shaped the words, "How much?"

"Two hundred pounds," was the answer.

Unconscious of his wife's shriek, the old man smiled faintly, put out his hands like a sightless man, and dropped, a senseless heap, to the floor.

III

In the huge new cemetery, some two miles distant, the old people buried their dead, and came back to a house steeped in shadow and silence. It was all over so quickly that at first they could hardly realize it, and remained in a state of expectation as though of something else to happen – something else which was to lighten this load, too heavy for old hearts to bear.

But the days passed, and expectation gave place to resignation – the hopeless resignation of the old, sometimes miscalled, apathy.[12] Sometimes they hardly exchanged a word, for now they had nothing to talk about, and their days were long to weariness.

It was about a week after that that the old man, waking suddenly in the night, stretched out his hand and found himself alone. The room was in darkness, and the sound of subdued weeping came from the window. He raised himself in bed and listened.

"Come back," he said tenderly. "You will be cold."

"It is colder for my son," said the old woman, and wept afresh.

The sound of her sobs died away on his ears. The bed was warm, and his eyes heavy with sleep. He dozed fitfully, and then slept until a sudden wild cry from his wife awoke him with a start.

"*The paw!*" she cried wildly. "The monkey's paw!"

He started up in alarm. "Where? Where is it? What's the matter?"

She came stumbling across the room toward him. "I want it," she said quietly. "You've not destroyed it?"

"It's in the parlour, on the bracket," he replied, marvelling. "Why?"

She cried and laughed together, and bending over, kissed his cheek.

"I only just thought of it," she said hysterically. "Why didn't I think of it before? Why didn't *you* think of it?"

"Think of what?" he questioned.

"The other two wishes," she replied rapidly. "We've only had one."

"Was not that enough?" he demanded fiercely.

---

[12] *apathy:* lack of interest in anything

"No," she cried, triumphantly; "we'll have one more. Go down and get it quickly, and wish our boy alive again."

The man sat up in bed and flung the bedclothes from his quaking limbs. "Good God, you are mad!" he cried aghast.

"Get it," she panted; "get it quickly, and wish – Oh, my boy, my boy!"

Her husband struck a match and lit the candle. "Get back to bed," he said, unsteadily. "You don't know what you are saying."

"We had the first wish granted," said the old woman, feverishly; "why not the second?"

"A coincidence," stammered the old man.

"Go and get it and wish," cried the old woman, quivering with excitement.

The old man turned and regarded her, and his voice shook. "He has been dead ten days, and besides he – I would not tell you else, but – I could only recognize him by his clothing. If he was too terrible for you to see then, how now?"

"Bring him back," cried the old woman, and dragged him toward the door. "Do you think I fear the child I have nursed?"

He went down in the darkness, and felt his way to the parlour, and then to the mantelpiece. The talisman was in its place, and a horrible fear that the unspoken wish might bring his mutilated[13] son before him ere he could escape from the room seized upon him, and he caught his breath as he found that he had lost the direction of the door. His brow cold with sweat, he felt his way round the table, and groped along the wall until he found himself in the small passage with the unwholesome thing in his hand.

---

[13] **mutilated:** horribly damaged

Even his wife's face seemed changed as he entered the room. It was white and expectant, and to his fears seemed to have an unnatural look upon it. He was afraid of her.

"*Wish!*" she cried, in a strong voice.

"It is foolish and wicked," he faltered.

"*Wish!*" repeated his wife.

He raised his hand. "I wish my son alive again."

The talisman fell to the floor, and he regarded it fearfully. Then he sank trembling into a chair as the old woman, with burning eyes, walked to the window and raised the blind.

He sat until he was chilled with the cold, glancing occasionally at the figure of the old woman peering through the window. The candle end, which had burnt below the rim of the china candlestick, was throwing pulsating shadows on the ceiling and walls, until, with a flicker larger than the rest, it expired. The old man, with an unspeakable sense of relief at the failure of the talisman, crept back to his bed, and a minute or two afterward the old woman came silently and apathetically beside him.

Neither spoke, but both lay silently listening to the ticking of the clock. A stair creaked, and a squeaky mouse scurried noisily through the wall. The darkness was oppressive, and after lying for some time screwing up his courage, the husband took the box of matches, and striking one, went downstairs for a candle.

At the foot of the stairs the match went out, and he paused to strike another, and at the same moment a knock, so quiet and stealthy as to be scarcely audible, sounded on the front door.

The matches fell from his hand. He stood motionless, his breath suspended until the knock was repeated. Then he turned and fled swiftly back to his room, and closed the door behind him. A third knock sounded through the house.

"*What's that?*" cried the old woman, starting up.

"A rat," said the old man, in shaking tones – "a rat. It passed me on the stairs."

His wife sat up in bed listening. A loud knock resounded through the house.

"It's Herbert!" she screamed. "It's Herbert!"

She ran to the door, but her husband was before her, and catching her by the arm, held her tightly.

"What are you going to do?" he whispered hoarsely.

"It's my boy; it's Herbert!" she cried, struggling mechanically. "I forgot it was two miles away. What are you holding me for? Let go. I must open the door."

"For God's sake, don't let it in," cried the old man trembling.

"You're afraid of your own son," she cried, struggling. "Let me go. I'm coming, Herbert; I'm coming."

There was another knock, and another. The old woman with a sudden wrench broke free and ran from the room. Her husband followed to the landing, and called after her appealingly as she hurried downstairs. He heard the chain rattle back and the bottom bolt drawn slowly and stiffly from the socket. Then the old woman's voice, strained and panting.

"The bolt," she cried loudly. "Come down. I can't reach it."

But her husband was on his hands and knees groping wildly on the floor in search of the paw. If he could only find it before the thing outside got in. A perfect fusillade[14] of knocks reverberated through the house, and he heard the scraping of a chair as his wife put it down in the passage against the door. He heard the creaking of the bolt as it came slowly back, and at the same moment he found the monkey's paw, and frantically breathed his third and last wish.

The knocking ceased suddenly, although the echoes of it were still in the house. He heard the chair drawn back and the door opened. A cold wind rushed up the staircase, and a long loud wail of disappointment and misery from his wife gave him courage to run down to her side, and then to the gate beyond. The street lamp flickering opposite shone on a quiet and deserted road.

---

[14] *fusillade*: rapid and constant series

Activities

Reading

I   Read the opening of the story until the arrival of Sergeant-Major Morris.
    What is the mood of the story at this stage?
2   Then read the last sentence. What is the mood at the close?
3   What are the first clues that this story is going to be sinister?
4   According to Morris, what was the purpose of the fakir's spell on the paw?
5   How does the author build up suspense in part III?

Language study

6   *The Monkey's Paw* was published in 1902. Collect as many examples of
    'old-fashioned' words and sentences from the text as you can.

Speaking and listening

7   Prepare to tell the story from Mr White's point of view. As well as
    recounting the main events in the correct order, you will need to include:
    ● his personal reactions to the events
    ● his final reflections (for example, what he now wishes or regrets).
8   Discuss why horror stories are so enduringly popular. Why do people enjoy
    stories that frighten them?
9   What would you consider to be the vital ingredients of a classic horror story?

Writing

10 "The bolt" she cried loudly. "Come down. I can't reach it." Use this as a
    starting point to write an alternative resolution to *The Monkey's Paw*. Your
    ending must resolve the return of the dead son and the third and final wish.
11 Write a letter from Mr or Mrs White to Sergeant-Major Morris giving a brief
    account of the events (but without telling everything) and the writer's
    comments about the powers of the paw and of fate.

Compare and contrast

12 Read *The Fisherman and the Jinnee* story (page 132). What similarities do
    you note in the structure of the two stories?

Further reading

You might like to read some other classic horror tales, such as *Ghost Tales*
by M.R. James, *Tales of Mystery and Imagination* by Edgar Allan Poe, *Best
Ghost Stories* by Charles Dickens, *Dracula* by Bram Stoker and *Frankenstein*
by Mary Shelley.

The Son Murdered by his Parents

Katharine Briggs and Ruth Tongue

This spooky tale is taken from Briggs and Tongue's vast collection of *British folk Tales*. The books record thousands of stories as they have been told all over the country – a wonderful resource for any storyteller!

A wayside cottage had belonged to two old people, who died, leaving it in very bad repair. Their only son had gone out, years before, to Australia, and no word had been heard from him since. So, after some time the cottage was done up, and new tenants moved in.

They found it impossible to live there though, because of the strange sounds they heard at night. So badly was it haunted that the parson was called in. His efforts were all in vain and it remained empty.

Then one day an old stranger woman came through the village selling brooms, and hearing of the haunted house, she offered to lay the spirit herself; all she asked was a fire in the room, a table and a chair, a Bible, and some sewing to busy her hands with. These she was gladly given, and she settled down to keep her lonely watch.

At midnight the door burst open, and in lurched – a monstrous pig! Laying her hand on the Holy Book, the old woman said, "Satan, depart, and let this spirit come back in its natural form." On this, the pig went out and a young man came in its place. And when told to "Speak in God's name," this is the story he told.

He was the missing son of the old people who had lived there. Out in Australia he had fallen on bad times, and for lack of any good news to send, he had not written home for years. Suddenly he struck gold, and having made his fortune, he decided to come home and give his parents a joyful surprise. He arrived at the town near his old home, too late to bank his money as he had intended, and took it with him as he walked out to his parents' cottage. When he got there and found that he had altered so much that his own parents did not recognize him, he carried on the joke, as he thought, by asking and obtaining a night's lodging, and listening over a scanty supper to their tale of poverty and distress. He went to bed, glad in his heart to think of the grand sensation he would cause when he revealed himself and his riches to them in the morning. But the old people, poor wretches, were even more desperate than he had realized. Somehow they had caught the gleam, and felt the weight of his gold, and falling under the dreadful temptation, they killed "the stranger" in his sleep, and buried him behind the house.

"Come," said the spirit, "and see where my bones lie. Let them be gathered, and laid in consecrated ground, and I will trouble this place no more." The old woman followed, and the spirit hovered over one particular spot in the garden, and then disappeared. Fearing lest she should not recognize the exact place by daylight, she took off the thimble which she was still wearing, and with it marked the place. Next day the ground was dug over, bones were found there and duly buried in the churchyard, after which the cottage remained as quiet at night as any other.

Activities

Reading

1 What sort of character is the 'old stranger woman'? Can you think of similar characters in other folk tales?

2 If this tale had a moral, what would it be?

3 Use the planning sheet on page 153 to analyse the structure of the story. Make brief notes on its setting, characters, problem, complications, resolution and ending.

Language study

4 This story takes place over a long time span. Collect a list of all the words and phrases that signal the passing of time, for example, paragraph 1: 'years before … after some time …'. (Note that these are all adverbial phrases as they provide information about when an action is being performed.)

5 Make a list of alternative adverbial phrases that could be inserted in the story to change the time span.

Speaking and listening

6 Prepare the telling of a ghost story. Think about the way a spoken story:
- involves the audience (for example, by addressing them directly, asking them questions)
- uses detail to set the mood.

Writing

7 Use the story planning sheet on page 153 to draw up the plan for your own ghost story. Note: One tip for writing a short story is to have only one problem – even if there are a number of complications.

Further reading

You might also like to read *The Shadow Cage and Other Tales of the Supernatural* by Philippa Pearce, *True Ghost Stories* by Terry Deary, *Selected British Folk Tales* by Kevin Crossley-Holland (read by Martin Jarvis in the audiobook format), and *A Dictionary of British Folk Tales in the English Language, Parts 1 & 2* by Katharine Briggs and Ruth Tongue.

Late

Carol Ann Duffy

Born in 1955, Carol Ann Duffy is currently one of the UK's leading poets. As well as writing poetry for readers of all ages, she regularly presents poetry programmes on the radio.

SHE was eight. She was out late.
She bounced a tennis ball homewards before her in the last of the light.
She'd been warned. She'd been told. It grew cold.
She took a shortcut through the churchyard.
She was a small child
making her way home. She was quite brave.
She fell into an open grave.

It was deep. It was damp. It smelled strange.
Help, she cried, Help, it's Me! She shouted her own name.
Nobody came.
The churchbells tolled sadly. Shame. Shame.

She froze. She had a blue nose.
She clapped her hands.
She stamped her feet in soft, slip-away soil.
She hugged herself. Her breath was a ghost floating up from a grave.
Then she prayed.

But only the moon stared down with its callous face.
Only the spiteful stars sniggered, far out in space.
Only the gathering clouds
threw down a clap of thunder
like an ace.
And her, she was eight, going on nine.
She was late.

Activities

Reading

1 Where was the child coming from?
2 'Her breath was a ghost flying up from the grave.' What is the effect of this image?

Language study

3 Look closely at the use of personification (the technique by which inanimate objects are described as if they were human) in the verbs used in the last verse, such as 'the moon *stared*'. Find and list other examples of personification. What is the impact of these verbs?

Speaking and listening

4 Hold a discussion on why you think the poet avoids giving the child a name.
5 The poem ends without a clear resolution. What do you think will happen to the child?

Writing

6 Write a short news report of this incident with the headline: Girl Found In Open Grave. Before writing, you will need to decide on the resolution (see above).

Further reading

You might like to read *Meeting Midnight* by Carol Ann Duffy.

An Arrest

Ambrose Bierce

The stories of Ambrose Bierce (1842–?1914) reflect his colourful life. Born in Ohio and raised on an Indiana farm, Bierce was the tenth of 13 children. He served in the American Civil War as a young man, and later prospected for gold, worked as a watchman and then became a well-known journalist in England, San Francisco and Washington. He earned the nickname 'Bitter Bierce' for the hard, acidic humour in his articles and short stories, but his output was prodigious and it has been said that he produced over three million words!

Eventually Bierce travelled to fight in the Mexican Civil War where he disappeared without trace.

An Arrest is a fine example of one of Bierce's tall tales from the old American West.

HAVING murdered his brother-in-law, Orrin Brower of Kentucky was a fugitive[1] from justice. From the county jail where he had been confined to await his trial he had escaped by knocking down his jailer with an iron bar, robbing him of his keys and, opening the outer door, walking out into the night. The jailer being unarmed, Brower got no weapon with which to defend his recovered liberty. As soon as he was out of the town he had the folly to enter a forest; this was many years ago, when that region was wilder than it is now.

---

[1] *fugitive:* someone who runs away

The night was pretty dark, with neither moon nor stars visible, and as Brower had never dwelt thereabout, and knew nothing of the lay of the land, he was, naturally, not long in losing himself. He could not have said if he were getting farther away from the town or going back to it – a most important matter to Orrin Brower. He knew that in either case a posse[2] of citizens with a pack of bloodhounds would soon be on his track and his chance of escape was very slender; but he did not wish to assist in his own pursuit. Even an added hour of freedom was worth having.

Suddenly he emerged from the forest into an old road, and there before him saw, indistinctly, the figure of a man, motionless in the gloom. It was too late to retreat: the fugitive felt that at the first movement back toward the wood he would be, as he afterwards explained, "filled with buckshot".[3] So the two stood there like trees, Brower nearly suffocated by the activity of his own heart; the other – the emotions of the other are not recorded.

A moment later – it may have been an hour – the moon sailed into a patch of unclouded sky and the hunted man saw the visible embodiment of Law[4] lift an arm and point significantly toward and beyond him. He understood. Turning his back to his captor, he walked submissively away in the direction indicated, looking to neither the right nor the left; hardly daring to breathe, his head and back actually aching with a prophecy of buckshot.

Brower was as courageous a criminal as ever lived to be hanged; that was shown by the conditions of awful personal

[2] *posse:* group
[3] *buckshot:* the shot used in shotguns
[4] *embodiment of Law:* physical presence of a police officer

peril in which he had coolly killed his brother-in-law. It is needless to relate them here; they came out at his trial, and the revelation of his calmness in confronting them came near to saving his neck. But what would you have – when a brave man is beaten, he submits.

So they pursued their journey jailward along the old road through the woods. Only once did Brower venture a turn of the head: just once, when he was in deep shadow and he knew that the other was in moonlight, he looked backward. His captor was Burton Duff, the jailer, as white as death and bearing upon his brow the livid mark of the iron bar. Orrin Brower had no further curiosity.

Eventually they entered the town, which was all alight, but deserted; only the women and children remained, and they were off the streets. Straight toward the jail the criminal held his way. Straight up to the main entrance he walked, laid his hand upon the knob of the heavy iron door, pushed it open without command, entered and found himself in the presence of a half-dozen armed men. Then he turned. Nobody else entered.

On a table in the corridor lay the dead body of Burton Duff.

Activities

Reading

1 Read the fifth paragraph closely. What words does Bierce use to describe Orrin Brower?
2 Why was the town deserted with 'women and children ... off the streets'?
3 What picture does this tale give us of crime and justice in Kentucky during the nineteenth century?

Language study

4 The first sentence begins with the adverbial clause 'Having murdered his brother-in-law'. What is the impact of that clause?
5 Write some other opening sentences beginning 'Having ..."

Speaking and listening

6 *An Arrest* is set in the 'Wild West' of the nineteenth century. What is its appeal to the modern reader?
7 The author seems only to criticize Brower for his 'folly' of going into the dense forest. Does that make the tale amoral?

Writing

8 *An Arrest* would make a gripping short film. Write a storyboard for the final shots of the film (for instance, the journey into the jailhouse).
9 Write an eyewitness statement by one of the armed men who saw Brower's return to the jail. Be as precise as you can about the details: for example, what happened; whether Brower was alone; Brower's attitude and any reaction to his re-arrest.

Further reading

You might like to read *The Complete Short Stories* of Ambrose Bierce, or listen to the audiotape *Classic Chilling Tales 3* published by Naxos Audio.

Reported Horror

"O woe is me,
To have seen what I have seen, see what I see!"
William Shakespeare, *Hamlet*

"I shudder to tell it."
Virgil, *The Aeneid*

"I will show you fear in a handful of dust."
T.S. Eliot, *The Wasteland*

from *King Oedipus*

Sophocles

The plays of Sophocles were written in the fifth century BC for performance in the vast open-air theatre in the city of Athens. Crowds of up to 17 000 spectators would watch tragedies selected for the city's annual festival.

King Oedipus presents an epic story of one man's struggle with the forces of his destiny. As a youth he is given the prophecy that he will grow up to murder his own father and marry his own mother. He runs away from his home city to escape this destiny and he travels to Thebes, where he is eventually made king. At the height of his power, Oedipus discovers the true story of his birth, adoption and subsequent fate – that his wife, Queen Jocasta, is in fact his natural mother and that he has mistakenly killed his own father.

When all these terrible truths are revealed, first Jocasta and then Oedipus leave the stage in despair. Eventually a Messenger returns to tell the citizens what he has witnessed.

MESSENGER:
The queen is dead.

CITIZEN:

Poor lady – how?

MESSENGER:
By her own hand. But you are spared the worst,
you never had to watch ... I saw it all,
and with all the memory that's in me
you will learn what that poor woman suffered.

Once she'd broken in through the gates,
dashing past us, frantic, whipped to fury,
ripping her hair out with both hands –
straight to her rooms she rushed, flinging herself
across the bridal-bed, doors slamming behind her –
once inside, she wailed for Laius, dead so long,
remembering how she bore his child long ago,
the life that rose up to destroy him, leaving
its mother to mother living creatures
with the very son she'd borne.
Oh how she wept, mourning the marriage-bed
where she let loose that double brood – monsters –
husband by her husband, children by her child.
And then –
but how she died is more than I can say. Suddenly
Oedipus burst in, screaming, he stunned us so
we couldn't watch her agony to the end,
our eyes were fixed on him. Circling
like a maddened beast, stalking, here, there,
crying out to us –
                    Give him a sword! His wife,
no wife, his mother, where can he find the mother earth
that cropped two crops at once, himself and all his
     children?
He was raging – one of the dark powers pointing the way,

none of us mortals crowding around him, no,
with a great shattering cry – someone, something leading
    him on –
he hurled at the twin doors and bending the bolts back
out of their sockets, crashed through the chamber.

And there we saw the woman hanging by the neck,
cradled high in a woven noose, spinning,
swinging back and forth. And when he saw her,
giving a low, wrenching sob that broke our hearts,
slipping the halter from her throat, he eased her down,
in a slow embrace he laid her down, poor thing ...
then, what came next, what horror we beheld!

He rips off her brooches, the long gold pins
holding her robes – and lifting them high,
looking straight up into the points,
he digs them down into the sockets of his eyes, crying, "You,
you'll see no more the pain I suffered, all the pain I caused!
Too long you looked on the ones you never should have seen,
blind to the ones you longed to see, to know! Blind
from this hour on! Blind in the darkness – blind!"
His voice like a dirge,[1] rising, over and over
raising the pins, raking them down his eyes.
And at each stroke blood spurts from the roots,
splashing his beard, a swirl of it, nerves and clots –
black hail of blood pulsing, gushing down.

These are the griefs that burst upon them both,
coupling man and woman. The joy they had so lately,

---

[1] **dirge:** chant for the dead

the fortune of their old ancestral house
was deep joy indeed. Now, in this one day,
wailing, madness and doom, death, disgrace,
all the griefs in the world that you can name,
all are theirs forever.

Activities

Reading

1 Find these lines in the extract: '... you never had to watch ...'. '... how she died is more than I can say ...' '... then, what came next, what horror we beheld!' What is the dramatic effect of these moments where the Messenger is almost unable to tell his story?

Language study

2 It was a convention of Greek tragedy that moments of extreme violence took place offstage and were reported by witnesses, like the Messenger in this scene. How is his report designed to make a dramatic impact? Find examples of:
   ● the details reported
   ● the language used including the active verbs used for the Queen's and Oedipus's actions
   ● the use of metaphor and simile
   ● the use of direct speech for Oedipus
   ● the contrast between the gentle and the violent actions
   ● the Messenger's personal comments on what he has seen.
   (See also questions 5 and 6 on page 110.)

3 *King Oedipus* was written about 2 500 years ago, yet it is still regularly performed in theatres. From this extract, can you explain why it still has appeal to modern audiences?

Speaking and listening

4 *King Oedipus* deals with very sensitive issues (patricide, suicide, incest, fate and destiny). Discuss the idea that there are some themes that are best left alone in drama.

Writing

5 Use your ideas from the discussion topic above to write an essay discussing the statement: Some subjects are too sensitive to be dealt with in plays or films. Your essay should:
   ● introduce and explain the statement
   ● outline arguments for both sides of the case
   ● come to a conclusion.

6 Write a tabloid newspaper report of this royal double death.

Further reading

You might like to read *Sophocles: The Three Theban Plays*, translated Robert Fagles.

from *Twenty Four Hours*

Margaret Mahy

Margaret Mahy was born in 1936 in Whakatane, New
Zealand. She worked as a librarian before becoming a full-
time writer. She has written picture books, novels for
children and young adults, as well as scripts for television.

The fast-living teenage characters in *Twenty Four
Hours* inhabit a strange twilight zone where the
boundaries between reality and imagination are blurred.
In this extract, Ursa, an enigmatic girl, reveals the dark
secret of her childhood.

"My dad was ..." she broke off, "Oh," she said at last,
smiling the sort of smile that lifts one corner of the
mouth and twists the other down, "he could be lovely ... he
was lovely, played games, joked, cuddled us, and rubbed us
with his bristly chin before he shaved. Mind you, he did
lose his temper from time to time. Mum called it 'getting
his Irish up', though Dad wasn't Irish in any way. We took it
for granted for years, though I think Leo and I were
beginning to understand there was something a bit
excessive – a bit *odd* ..." She paused, then began again
briskly. "One night, Dad woke us all up – Leona, me, Wolf
and Felix ..."

"Wolf and Felix?" Ellis said uncertainly.

"My brothers," said Ursa. "There were five of us back
then. "We're going to look at the stars," my father said. "I've
got a telescope, and it's a lovely night." He made Leo carry

Fox, while he carried the telescope – it could easily have been a telescope – wrapped in a bit of sacking.

"So off we all went towards our front door. Mind you, I don't think any of us *really* thought we were going to look at the stars ... well, Felix might have, and Fox was only a baby. But Leo, Wolf and I knew that something else was going on. Hard to tell now, because you know how memories keep on shifting and changing. Anyhow, as we crossed the sitting room to the front door, I looked across into the kitchen. The door was partly open and I could make out bare legs, and the edge of my mother's dressing gown, and her feet, one with a slipper on and the other bare. My father saw me notice, but he just smiled. "It's a game, sweetheart ... don't worry, it's just a game," he said.

"So we went over the road to the cemetery – in at the gate we used today. And we stopped close to Rose Phipps – she was our Phippo's great-grandmother, may she rest in pieces! We stood there in the night. It wasn't dark. It never is, is it, in the centre of the city? That's why we couldn't really have looked at the stars.

" 'Life is too terrible to be lived,' my father said, out there among the tombstones. Of course, it wasn't a telescope he had in that sackcloth. It was a gun. Leo says she knew right then what he was going to do, even though she couldn't actually see the gun. She screamed at him and tried to hide Fox. But, before her scream was properly over, my father had shot Wolf and then Felix ..." Ursa scratched her head, looking at Ellis and pulling a rueful face. "Leo was hugging Fox like she hugged Shelley last night, sort of arching over her, doing everything she could to hide her. And Dad stood looking down at us, as if we were the ones who had done it all. We were yelling our heads off by then, and Dad was saying, 'Shh! Shh! Shh!' louder and louder – like an old steam train shunting. Then, suddenly, he – he just put the barrel of the gun in his own mouth and pulled the trigger."

Ursa stopped talking. They stared at each other.

Activities

Reading

1 How does Ursa remember her father?
2 What clues are given about the father's state of mind that night?
3 What was the first sign to the child that everything was not right that night?
4 Ursa recounts the events without revealing her feelings about them. Why do you think that is?

Language study

5 Can you explain the author's choice of two very short sentences at the end of the extract and the effect they have? Find where else in this extract the writer has used a very short sentence and explain why it is effective.
6 It would normally be regarded as poor English to begin sentences with conjunctions, however the writer does so deliberately a number of times in this extract. Looking at page 108, pick out where this has been done, then try to explain why it is appropriate here.

Compare and contrast

7 Compare this with the extract from *King Oedipus* (page 102). Compare the way the two witnesses describe the horrific events. Which one has the greater impact on the reader?

Writing

8 Choose the extract you judge to have the most impact. Write a review of the text, explaining its effect. Refer to quotes from the text to support your judgements.

Further reading

You might like to read *Twenty four Hours* and *The Haunting*, both by Margaret Mahy.

A Twist in the Tale

There is a special pleasure to be had from a story that builds up to a surprising or ironic resolution. Whether it is the triumph of a trickster, a cruel twist of fate or just deserts for everyone, a neat ending is always satisfying.

This section contains a range of stories from different cultures, all of which conclude with ironic twists.

The Goat and the Ass

Aesop

A goat and an ass were kept by the same master. The goat was jealous of the ass because he had food enough and to spare. "Your life is an unending toil," she said to him, "what with turning the millstone and carrying loads. I advise you to pretend to have a fit and tumble into a hole, so that you can have a rest." The ass took her advice, and was seriously injured by his fall. So the master sent for the veterinary surgeon and requested his help. He prescribed broth made from a goat's lung, which he said would effect a cure. So they butchered the goat to doctor the ass.

Activities

Reading

1 Fables like this often have a moral at the end. Supply the moral to this fable.
2 Fables often use animals as their characters. How does this help the stories to work?
3 The story sets up the characters, setting and problem inside two short sentences. How has the writer achieved this? (Look closely at the way the sentences are written.)

Writing

4 All the stories in this section end with an ironic twist, but this is by far the shortest. Write a short story that ends with an ironic resolution, for example, some person or creature caught out by their own trick. Edit and revise your work to cut it down to the minimum number of words.
5 Write a modern-day fable. Start with the moral and then devise a simple tale to bear it out.

Further reading

You might like to read *Aesop – The Complete Fables*, translated Robert and Olivia Temple.

Alternatively, there are many on-line collections of Aesop on the internet.

The Huntsman

Edward Lowbury

Edward Lowbury (born 1913) had a distinguished medical career as a pathologist. As well as medical writing, he has written biographies and poetry.

The Huntsman recasts as a poem a tale he heard whilst travelling in Kenya in 1944.

KAGWA hunted the lion,
Through bush and forest went his spear.
One day he found the skull of a man
    And said to it, "How did you come here?"
The skull opened its mouth and said
    "Talking brought me here."

Kagwa hurried home;
    Went to the king's chair and spoke:
"In the forest I found a talking skull."
    The king was silent. Then he said slowly
"Never since I was born of my mother
    Have I seen or heard of a skull which spoke."

The king called out his guards:
    "Two of you now go with him
And find this talking skull:
    But if his tale is a lie
And the skull speaks no word,
    This Kagwa himself must die."

They rode into the forest:
    For days and nights they found nothing.
At last they saw the skull; Kagwa
    Said to it "How did you come here?"
The skull said nothing. Kagwa implored,
    But the skull said nothing.

The guards said "Kneel down."
    They killed him with a sword and spear.
Then the skull opened its mouth;
    "Huntsman, how did you come here?"
And the dead man answered
    "Talking brought me here."

Activities

Reading
1 What was Kagwa's big mistake?
2 Why did he make that mistake?
3 Compare the first and last stanzas of the poem. Why do you think the first verse is echoed at the end?

Speaking and listening
4 The story began as an oral tale before Lowbury retold it in verse. Work in a group to prepare a dramatic presentation of the poem. You will need to think about:
  ● the dramatic technique to create the talking skull
  ● the use of sound/light to make the ending effective.

Writing
5 The ironic ending means that Kagwa learns his lesson too late. Plan and write your own story in which someone learns the truth too late to help themselves. This could be written in the form of a poem.

Further reading

You might like to read *The Oxford Book of Story Poems*, eds Harrison and Stuart-Clark.
  The internet also provides many sites containing African folk tales.

The Happy Man's Shirt

Italo Calvino

Italo Calvino (1923–1985) wrote stories, essays and novels,
as well as putting together a vast collection of folktales
from all the regions of Italy.

A king had an only son that he thought the world of. But
this prince was always unhappy. He would spend days
on end at his window staring into space.

"What on earth do you lack?" asked the king. "What's
wrong with you?"

"I don't even know myself, Father."

"Are you in love? If there's a particular girl you fancy, tell
me, and I'll arrange for you to marry her, no matter
whether she's the daughter of the most powerful king on
earth or the poorest girl alive!"

"No, Father, I'm not in love."

The king tried in every way imaginable to cheer him up,
but theatres, balls, concerts and singing were all useless,
and day by day the rosy hue drained from the prince's face.

The king issued a decree,[1] and from every corner of the
earth came the most learned philosophers, doctors and
professors. The king showed them the prince and asked for
their advice. The wise men withdrew to think, then
returned to the king. "Majesty, we have given the matter
close thought and we have studied the stars. Here's what

---

[1] *decree:* law

you must do. Look for a happy man, a man who's happy through and through, and exchange your son's shirt for his."

That same day the king sent ambassadors to all parts of the world in search of the happy man.

A priest was taken to the king. "Are you happy?" asked the king.

"Yes, indeed, Majesty."

"Fine. How would you like to be my bishop?"

"Oh, Majesty, if only it were so!"

"Away with you! Get out of my sight! I'm seeking a man who's happy just as he is, not one who's trying to better his lot."

Thus the search resumed, and before long the king was told about a neighbouring king, who everybody said was a truly happy man. He had a wife as good as she was beautiful and a whole slew of children. He had conquered all his enemies, and his country was at peace. Again hopeful, the king immediately sent ambassadors to him to ask for his shirt.

The neighbouring king received the ambassadors and said, "Yes, indeed, I have everything anybody could possibly want. But at the same time I worry I'll have to die one day and leave it all. I can't sleep at night for worrying about that!" The ambassadors thought it wiser to go home without this man's shirt.

At his wit's end, the king went hunting. He fired at a hare but only wounded it, and the hare scampered away on three legs. The king pursued it, leaving the hunting party far behind him. Out in the open field he heard a man singing a refrain. The king stopped in his tracks. "Whoever sings like that is bound to be happy!" The song led him into a vineyard, where he found a young man singing and pruning the vines.

"Good day, Majesty," said the youth. "So early and already out in the country?"

"Bless you! Would you like me to take you to the capital? You will be my friend."

"Much obliged, Majesty, but I wouldn't even consider it. I wouldn't even change places with the Pope."

"Why not? Such a fine young man like you ..."

"No, no, I tell you. I'm content with just what I have and want nothing more."

"A happy man at last!" thought the king. "Listen, young man. Do me a favour."

"With all my heart, Majesty, if I can."

"Wait just a minute," said the king, who, unable to contain his joy any longer, ran to get his retinue. "Come with me! My son is saved! My son is saved! And he took them to the young man. "My dear lad," he began, "I'll give you whatever you want! But give me ... give me ..."

"What, Majesty?"

"My son is dying! Only you can save him. Come here!"

The king grabbed him and started unbuttoning the youth's jacket. All of a sudden he stopped, and his arms fell to his sides.

The happy man wore no shirt.

Activities

Reading

1 What is the flaw in the wisdom of the wise men?

2 What advice would be more useful for the unhappy prince?

Language study

3 The writer uses a variety of sentence structures including complex sentences like the one below which is made up of a main clause and a subordinate clause: 'Thus the search resumed, and before long the king was told about a neighbouring king, who everybody said was a truly happy man.' Reread the next but one paragraph that begins, 'At his wit's end ... Using punctuation (commas or semi-colons), conjunctions or link words to do with time ('later', 'until', 'before long'), try to rewrite the paragraph using complex sentences. Remember, a complex sentence will have a main clause and one or more subordinate clauses.

Speaking and listening

4 Discuss whether you would call this a wise tale.

5 Work with a partner to role-play a radio 'phone-in' programme where the unhappy prince (or his father) is asking for advice from an 'agony aunt'.

Writing

6 Write a modern version of this tale which keeps the same structure and outcome. You will need to update the characters, setting and language.

Compare and contrast

7 Read the traditional Zen tale of *Samurai and Hakuin* (page 141). Compare the way the central characters discover the answers to their questions.

Further reading

You might also like to read *Italian Folktales* by Italo Calvino and *The Decameron* by Boccaccio, translated by G.H. McWilliam for other Italian tales.

For folktales on the internet, use a search engine to visit 'Folklore and Mythology: Electronic Texts'. This site provides an extensive collection categorized by themes and countries of origin.

Bottles

David Greygoose

David Greygoose is a well-known poet who has written many poems for children. Often quirky and humorous, his work challenges the reader on many levels.

E ACH of the bottles is filled with water.
This is important to remember.
They may bear different names on the labels.
They may appear to be different colours.
But each of the bottles is filled with water.
They stand in a line on a stall
in the far corner of the market.

The first woman comes,
and buys one of the bottles.
She thinks the bottle contains wine.
She takes it home to drink with her husband.
They end the night tipsy with ecstasy, falling
into each other's arms.

The second woman comes,
and buys the second bottle.
She thinks the bottle contains perfume.
She takes it home and sprinkles it
on her arms and on her neck.
She smiles at the men who smile at her,
thinking they can smell the scent
that she cannot smell.

The third woman comes,
and buys the third bottle.
She thinks the bottle contains medicine.
She takes it home and gives a spoonful
to each of her sick children.
The next day their eyes are laughing
as they sing and play in the street.

The fourth woman comes,
and asks for water.
The stall-keeper shrugs and points at the labels.
The woman unscrews the largest bottle, the one
with the water dyed the most exotic colour,
the one with the highest price on the label.

"I'll take this one," she says, and stands
where she is and drinks every drop.
The stall-keeper, brazen-faced, still asks
for his money.
The woman bends down and picks up a stone.
"Here is a loaf of bread," she says.

Activities

Reading
1 What would make a good 'moral' for this story?
2 The poem begins with the writer addressing the reader directly. How does this affect the way the story works?

Language study
3 The poem tells the story in the present tense (for example, 'The first woman comes ...'). Why do you think the poet has chosen to write in this tense?

Speaking and listening
4 Retell the story of *The Bottles* as a joke. To involve your audience more you may need to:
   ● include direct speech
   ● exaggerate the imagined effect of the bottles
   ● think about the best way to deliver the 'punchline'.
5 The poem suggests that the power of alcohol, perfume and medicine can sometimes be 'all in the mind'. Do you think there is any truth in this? Could it be true for other products? Discuss these ideas.

Writing
6 Write alternative verses beginning with the lines:
   The _____ woman comes,
   and buys the _____ bottle.
   She thinks it contains _____
   She takes it home and _____
   Think of a new substance and explain its imagined effect on her life.
7 Write your own folktale in which a confidence trick is exposed. In the course of the tale address your reader directly (as David Greygoose does in the first verse). Share with your reader something that the characters in the story do not know.

An Aeroplane Journey

John Hegley

John Hegley (born 1953) is a poet, comedian, singer and radio performer. He began his career on the stand-up comedy circuit and he still regularly performs his poetry and songs to live audiences.

HE threw it at her in school assembly. He had assembled it during the sports notices. A page from the hymn book. It was her look he was after. Her look.

In his lap he flipped the tightly printed page into the tightly folded plane. She was in his head ninety-five per cent of his waking day and sixty-five per cent of his dreaming night. Sometimes he'd wanted to scream his fat infatuation when she was near and sometimes he'd wanted to whisper it in her ear so gentle. Instead he'd put his energies into keeping a stifled mask of no interest whatsoever. Fear of rejection? Or just fear? Whatever it was, it was fearful. Now he was going to throw down the mask. He was going to let the throwing of the plane do the asking. "How about a date? You're great!" he'd written in the top margin and signed it.

Heads down for silent prayer; he knew that would be his moment. He took careful aim.

Fly! fly little arrow to my heart's desire. To the source of this fire, fly, fly little arrow down a narrow corridor straight to your target. And the air was ridden and the message ended up where bidden. Silent, swift, unnoticed by the sundry and the all, falling, nestling in her spectacles. She took hold of the piece of paper and immediately caught sight of the handwriting so boldly put upon the wing. The name was a shock for sure. His dissembling[1] had covered up his wonderment so well. She hadn't been able to tell a single bubble of the cauldron burning up inside him. But she knew now. She knew just how the chemistry master felt about her. And she was a very happy head teacher indeed.

---

[1] *dissembling:* acting

Activities

Reading

1 Why does the writer conceal the identity of the two characters until the very end?

2 We are told of the cauldron bubbling up inside the man. Make a list of all the different emotions assigned to him.

3 Provide an alternative title for this story.

Language study

4 Read the fourth paragraph from 'Fly! fly little arrow' to 'ended up where bidden'. What do you notice about the language used in these sentences? What does it remind you of?

Speaking and listening

5 With a partner, look back over the extracts in this section and at the twist in each ending. Discuss which you found most effective and why. Are they all designed with the same purpose in mind, do you think, or can you discern different effects achieved by each ending?

Writing

6 Plan and write a short recount which conceals the surprising identity of the main character/s until the very end. It may help you to plan backwards. Start by deciding on your character and then describe them in an unlikely situation. As with *An Aeroplane Journey*, start the narrative in the middle of the action.

Further reading

You might like to read *Beyond Our Kennel* and *Dog*, both by John Hegley, or visit John Hegley's website.

Three Trickster Tales

How the Wicked Sons Were Duped

Traditional Indian Tale

A very wealthy old man, imagining that he was on the point of death, sent for his sons and divided his property among them. However, he did not die for several years afterwards; and miserable years many of them were. Besides the weariness of old age, the old fellow had to bear with much abuse and cruelty from his sons. Wretched, selfish ingrates![1] Previously they vied with one another in trying to please their father, hoping thus to receive more money, but now they had received their patrimony,[2] they cared not how soon he left them – nay, the sooner the better, because he was only a needless trouble and expense. This, as we may suppose, was a great grief to the old man. One day he met a friend and related to him all his troubles. The friend sympathized very much with him, and promised to think over the matter, and call in a little while and tell him what to do. He did so; in a few days he visited the old man and put down four bags full of stones and gravel before him.

"Look here, friend," said he. "Your sons will get to know

---

[1] **ingrates:** ungrateful people
[2] **patrimony:** inheritance from father

of my coming here today, and will inquire about it. You must pretend that I came to discharge a long-standing debt with you, and that you are several thousands of rupees richer that you thought you were. Keep these bags in your own hands, and on no account let your sons get to them as long as you are alive. You will soon find them change their conduct towards you. *Salám.* I will come again soon to see how you are getting on."

When the young men got to hear of this further increase of wealth they began to be more attentive and pleasing to their father than ever before. And thus they continued to the day of the old man's demise,[3] when the bags were greedily opened, and found to contain only stones and gravel!

Drinking Poison

Traditional Vietnamese Tale

THERE was a rich man who had a passion for rice wine, but he never gave any to his servant. Not even a small cupful at *Tet.*

He had to be away from home one day, so he gave instructions to the servant: "While I'm absent you must watch over the rooster in the cage, and that fine piece of pork in the kitchen. Don't let the cat or the dog go near them." He pointed to a bottle of his favourite rice wine on the shelf and warned, "That's a bottle of poison I bought to kill the rats. Whatever you do, don't drink it."

---

[3] ***demise:*** death

As soon as the rich man had departed the servant killed the rooster, and cooked it and the pork for his lunch. He washed it down with the rice wine and had the most splendid meal he had ever tasted.

The master arrived home and found his servant in a drunken sleep on the kitchen floor. He shook him awake and demanded to know what had happened to the rooster and the pork, and why he had drunk from the bottle.

"Oh, great lord," sobbed the servant, "I did my best to guard your food but the cat managed to steal the pork and the dog killed the rooster. I was so afraid of your anger that I decided to kill myself and drank the poison. Oh, unlucky me, I am still alive."

The Feast

Traditional African Tale

ONE day a wealthy chief decided to hold a magnificent feast for his people. Everyone in the village was invited and each family was asked to bring with them a jug of palm wine.

The day of the great feast arrived and there was much excitement in the village. People put on their best clothes and walked with their families to the chief's house. At the door they were asked to pour their palm wine into a large pot. But there was one man who did not have any wine and when his wife suggested that he go to buy some from a friend, he replied, "Buy wine? For a feast where I'm a guest? No chance of that! I've a far better idea."

The man's plan was to take along a jug of water and pour that into the jug at the door. "After all," he reckoned, "there are hundreds of jugs of wine in there. No one will ever taste just one drop of water in so much wine."

When he arrived at the chief's house, the man joined the line, waited his turn and poured his water into the great pot of palm wine before taking his place with all the other guests. The chief ordered the cups to be filled and invited his guests to drink with him.

All the guests raised their glasses and drank. They looked puzzled and drank again. For what they were drinking was not palm wine, but water from the village spring. You see, everybody had had the same idea and everybody had thought a little drop of water would not be tasted in so much wine. The great pot contained water and nothing else.

Activities

Reading

I   Which of the three tricksters is the most appealing character? Why?

Speaking and listening

2   Trickster tales are common in all cultures, and they often feature in modern jokes and cartoons. Can you think of any examples that you have read or seen?

3   What is it that we enjoy about trickster tales?

Writing

4   Use the story planner (page 153) to plan a trickster tale. When you have worked out the trick that will resolve the tale, aim to hide it from the reader until as late as possible.

5   Now either write your planned tale as a story or present it in cartoon form using speech and thought bubbles.

6   Choose one of the tricksters. Imagine that he was put on trial for his offence and write a speech to the court to defend him. He might be guilty but you can still give an argument for his sentence to be light.

Further reading

You might like to read *The Illustrated Anansi* by Philip Sherlock and Petrina Wright for stories about a famous trickster in Caribbean and African folklore, the spiderman Anansi. Also, *A Treasury of Trickster Tales* by Valerie Marsh and Patrick K. Luzadder contains many lively and interesting stories.

For trickster tales on the internet, enter 'Anansi' or 'Coyote' into a search engine.

Magical Tales

"The realm of fairy story is ... filled with many things: all manner of beasts and birds are found there; shoreless seas and stars uncounted; beauty that is an enchantment, and an ever-present peril; both joy and sorrow sharp as swords."   J.R.R. Tolkien

The Fisherman and the Jinnee

Arabian Nights

O NCE upon a time there was a poor fisherman who had a wife and three children to support.

He used to cast his net four times a day. It chanced that one day he went down to the sea at noon and, reaching the shore, set down his basket, rolled up his shirt-sleeves, and cast his net far out into the water. After he had waited for it to sink, he pulled on the cords with all his might; but the net was so heavy that he could not draw it in. So he tied the rope ends to a wooded stake on the beach and, putting off his clothes, dived into the water and set to work to bring it up. When he had carried it ashore, however, he found in it a dead donkey.

"By Allah, this is a strange catch!" cried the fisherman, disgusted at the sight. After he had freed the net and wrung it out, he waded into the water and cast it again, invoking Allah's help. But when he tried to draw it in he found it even heavier than before. Thinking that he had caught some enormous fish, he fastened the ropes to the stake and, diving in again, brought up the net. This time he found a large earthen vessel filled with mud and sand.

Angrily the fisherman threw away the vessel, cleaned his net, and cast it for the third time. He waited patiently, and when he felt the net grow heavy he hauled it in, only to find it filled with bones and broken glass. In despair, he lifted his eyes to heaven and cried: "Allah knows that I cast my net only four times a day. I have already cast it for the third time and caught no fish at all. Surely He will not fail me again!"

With this the fisherman hurled his net far out into the sea, and waited for it to sink to the bottom. When at length he brought it to land he found in it a bottle made of yellow copper. The mouth was stopped with lead and bore the seal of our master Solomon son of David. The fisherman rejoiced, and said: "I will sell this in the market of the coppersmiths. It must be worth ten pieces of gold." He shook the bottle and, finding it heavy, thought to himself: "I will first break the seal and find out what is inside."

The fisherman removed the lead with his knife and again shook the bottle; but scarcely had he done so, when there burst from it a great column of smoke which spread along the shore and rose so high that it almost touched the heavens. Taking shape, the smoke resolved itself into a jinnee of such prodigious stature[1] that his head reached the clouds, while his feet were planted on the sand. His head was a huge dome and his mouth as wide as a cavern, with teeth ragged like broken rocks. His legs towered like the masts of a ship, his nostrils were two inverted bowls, and his eyes, blazing like torches, made his aspect fierce and menacing.

The sight of this jinnee[2] struck terror into the fisherman's heart; his limbs quivered, his teeth chattered together, and he stood rooted to the ground with parched tongue and staring eyes.

"There is no god but Allah and Solomon is His Prophet!" cried the jinnee. Then, addressing himself to the fisherman,

---

[1] *prodigious stature:* enormous size
[2] *jinnee:* spirit in human form

he said: "I pray you, mighty Prophet, do not kill me! I swear never again to defy your will or violate your laws!"

"Blasphemous giant," cried the fisherman, "do you presume to call Solomon the Prophet of Allah? Solomon has been dead these eighteen hundred years, and we are now approaching the end of Time. But what is your history, pray, and how came you to be imprisoned in this bottle?"

On hearing these words the jinnee replied sarcastically: "Well, then; there is no god but Allah! Fisherman, I bring you good news."

"What news?" asked the old man.

"News of your death, horrible and prompt!" replied the jinnee.

"Then may heaven's wrath be upon you, ungrateful wretch!" cried the fisherman. "Why do you wish my death, and what have I done to deserve it? Have I not brought you up from the depths of the sea and released you from your imprisonment?"

But the jinnee answered: "Choose the manner of your death and the way that I shall kill you. Come, waste no time!"

"But what crime have I committed?" cried the fisherman.

"Listen to my story, and you shall know," replied the jinnee.

"Be brief, then, I pray you," said the fisherman, "for you have wrung my soul with terror."

"Know," began the giant, "that I am one of the rebel jinn[3] who, together with Sakhr the Jinnee, mutinied against Solomon son of David. Solomon sent against me his Vizier,[4]

---

[3] *jinn:* plural of jinnee
[4] *vizier:* high official

Asaf ben Berakhya, who vanquished me despite my supernatural power and led me captive before his master. Invoking the name of Allah, Solomon adjured me to embrace his faith and pledge him absolute obedience. I refused, and he imprisoned me in this bottle, upon which he set a seal of lead bearing the Name of the Most High. Then he sent for several of his faithful jinn, who carried me away and cast me into the middle of the sea. In the ocean depths I vowed: "I will bestow eternal riches on him who sets me free!" But a hundred years passed away and no one freed me. In the second hundred years of my imprisonment I said: "For him who frees me I will open up the buried treasures of the earth!" And yet no one freed me. Whereupon I flew into a rage and swore: "I will kill the man who sets me free, allowing him only to choose the manner of his death!" Now it was you who set me free: therefore prepare to die and choose the way that I shall kill you."

"O wretched luck, that it should have fallen to my lot to free you!" exclaimed the fisherman. "Spare me, almighty jinnee, and Allah will spare you; kill me, and so shall Allah destroy you!"

"You have freed me," repeated the jinnee. "Therefore you must die."

"Chief of the jinn," cried the fisherman, "will you thus requite good with evil?"

"Enough of this talk!" roared the jinnee. "Kill you I must."

At this point the fisherman thought to himself: "Though I am but a man and he is a jinnee, my cunning may yet over-reach his malice." Then, turning to his adversary,[5] he said:

---

[5] *adversary:* opponent

"Before you kill me, I beg you in the Name of the Most High engraved on Solomon's seal to answer me one question truthfully."

The jinnee trembled at the mention of the Name, and, when he had promised to answer truthfully, the fisherman asked: "How could this bottle, which is scarcely large enough to hold your hand or foot, ever contain your entire body?"

"Do you dare doubt that?" roared the jinnee indignantly.

"I will never believe it," replied the fisherman, "until I see you enter this bottle with my own eyes!"

Upon this the jinnee trembled from head to foot and dissolved into a column of smoke, which gradually wound itself into the bottle and disappeared inside. At once the fisherman snatched up the leaden stopper and thrust it into the mouth of the bottle. Then he called out to the jinnee: "Choose the manner of your death and the way that I shall kill you! By Allah, I will throw you back into the sea, and keep watch on this shore to warn all men of your treachery!"

When he heard the fisherman's words, the jinnee struggled desperately to escape from the bottle, but was prevented by the magic seal. He now altered his tone and, assuming a submissive air, assured the fisherman that he had been jesting with him and implored him to let him out. But the fisherman paid no heed to the jinnee's entreaties, and resolutely carried the bottle down to the sea.

Urashima and the Turtle

Traditional Japanese Tale

L ONG ago there lived a fisherman named Urashima. He lived at home with his mother, for he was unmarried. When she urged him to find a bride, he answered, "I can only catch enough fish to feed two, so while you are alive I will not marry."

One day, all he caught was a little turtle. "You will scarcely make a mouthful for mother and a mouthful for me," he said.

The turtle replied, "In that case, set me free! If you show me mercy, I will show you gratitude." Kind-hearted Urashima set the turtle free.

Several years later, when Urashima was out fishing as usual, a storm swept through the bay and capsized his boat. Like so many fishermen, he could not swim, and he seemed sure to drown. But as he splashed and spluttered, a huge turtle swam up from the depths. "I am the turtle whose life you once saved," it said. "Climb on my back."

The turtle did not take Urashima to the shore – it plunged down, down to Ryugu, the dragon king's palace at the bottom of the sea. "I am maid-in-waiting to the Dragon Princess Otohime," the turtle said. "She wishes to thank you herself for saving my life."

As soon as they set eyes on each other, Urashima and the princess fell in love. She begged him to stay, telling him, "In this kingdom you will never grow old."

Three years passed and Urashima and the princess were

very happy. Just one thing spoiled Urashima's contentment – worry about his mother. One day he asked Princess Otohime if he could visit her.

"If you go," she replied sadly, "you will not return." Urashima pleaded and at least she gave in. She placed a small casket in his hand, saying, "Keep this safe, and never open it. If you do this, the turtle will meet you at the seashore and bring you back to me."

Urashima promised not to open the box. He seated himself on the turtle's back and the creature took him back to the beach he knew so well. But everything had changed. As he walked through his village, Urashima could not see anyone or anything he recognized. Where his home had been, only the stone washbasin and the garden steps remained. After a while he asked an old man if he had ever heard of a fisherman named Urashima.

"Don't you know the legend?" the old man replied. "It's said that Urashima lived in this village three hundred years ago, but he went down to the dragon kingdom under the sea and never came back."

"What happened to his mother?" asked Urashima.

"She died the day he left," the old man replied.

Urashima could not believe his ears. "I am Urashima," he cried, "and I've only been away three years, not three hundred!"

He took out the box, saying, "Look, this was a parting gift from the dragon princess." In his haste, he forgot the dragon princess's warning, and opened the box. There was nothing in it but a puff of smoke. And as the smoke escaped, the weight of years fell on Urashima. His skin wrinkled, his legs gave way, and his body crumbled to dust.

Activities

Language study

1 The extract, *The Fisherman and the Jinnee*, from *The Thousand and One Nights* (or *The Arabian Nights*) was translated into English in 1954. It deliberately uses archaic (old-fashioned) words and sentence structures. Find examples of these. How do they contribute to the impact of the story?

Speaking and listening

2 Apart from magic, what are the traditional features of fairytales? Discuss with your group.

3 Take some of those 'ingredients' and create the opening of a traditional fairytale. Establish the central character and their problem.

Writing

4 Now write your fairytale opening, using the language and style of a traditional tale.

5 Write an essay discussing these two views. Refer to famous tales as you consider both sides of the argument.

Fairytales are for kids. Magical spells, witches, princes and princesses have no place in the twenty-first century. People nowadays need more realistic stories.	Fairytales speak to our imaginations. They echo our dreams, hopes and fears. That's why we still tell them.

Compare and contrast

6 Both tales deal with a poor fisherman. What other similarities can you find?

7 Though the world of each tale is ruled by magic, characters also make choices and mistakes. What are the mistakes made by:
- the Jinnee?
- Urashima?

Further reading

You might like to read *Tales From The Thousand and One Nights*, translated by N.J. Dawood and *The Illustrated Book of Fairy Tales* by Neil Philip. Alternatively, you can find traditional tales on the internet.

The Moral of the Story

"Stories are the secret reservoir of values: change the stories individuals or nations live by and tell themselves and you change the individuals and nations.

Nations and peoples are largely the stories they feed themselves. If they tell themselves stories that are lies, they will suffer the future consequences of those lies. If they tell themselves stories that face their own truths, they will free their histories for future flowerings."

Ben Okri, *Birds of Heaven*, Phoenix 1996

Samurai and Hakuin

Traditional Zen Buddhist Tale

The teachings of the Zen Buddhist priest Hakuin often come in the form of enigmatic stories.

A samurai warrior[1] came to the master Hakuin and asked, "Master, tell me, is there really such a thing as paradise or hell?"

The Master sat in silence, gazing all the while at his visitor. After a while he asked, "Who are you?"

"I am a samurai swordsman, and a member of the emperor's personal guard."

"You are a samurai?" Hakuin said doubtfully. "You look more like a beggar!"

"What?" the samurai stammered furiously, growing red in the face and reaching for his sword.

"Oho!" said Hakuin. "So you have a sword, do you! I'll bet it's not even sharp enough to cut off my little finger!"

The samurai was no longer able to control his anger. He drew his sword and readied to strike the master.

Hakuin responded quickly, "That is hell!"

The samurai, understanding the truth in the master's words and the risk he had taken, sheathed his sword and bowed.

"Now," said the master, "that is paradise."

---

[1] **samurai warrior:** Japenese soldier

Activities

Reading
1 For a long while Hakuin 'sat in silence'. What does this imply about him?
2 Do you think that the wise man has fully answered the warrior's question?

Language study
3 A simple tale such as this relies on careful use of language to 'paint' the scene. Try replacing the verbs such as 'said', 'responded' and 'stammered', firstly with alternatives that would fit with the original mood and events, then with ones that would change the mood drastically.
4 Perform the alternative versions in pairs to see the difference the choice of a verb can make!

Speaking and listening
5 Prepare questions to put to the samurai warrior about his visit to the wise teacher and what it has meant to him. Then hotseat one member of the group to answer the questions in role as the warrior.

Writing
6 Rewrite the story in the first person from the point of the view of the samurai warrior. As well as recounting the events and the conversation, he should also attempt to pass on what he has learned to the reader.

Further reading

You might like to read *Wisdom Tales from Around the World* by Heather Forest, or visit the 'Wisdom Tales' website.

Parable of the Vineyard Labourers

Matthew 20 v.1–16

This parable is taken from the New English Bible translation of the gospel of St Matthew. Here Jesus uses a story to explain to his followers one idea of Heaven.

THE kingdom of Heaven is like this. There was once a landowner who went out early one morning to hire labourers for his vineyard; and after agreeing to pay them the usual day's wage he sent them off to work. Going out three hours later he saw some more men standing idle in the market-place. "Go and join the others in the vineyard," he said, "and I will pay you a fair wage"; so off they went. At noon he went out again, and at three in the afternoon, and made the same arrangement as before. An hour before sunset he went out and found another group standing there; so he said to them, "Why are you standing about like this all day with nothing to do?" "Because no one has hired us," they replied; so he told them, "Go and join the others in the vineyard." When evening fell, the owner of the vineyard said to his steward, "Call the labourers and give them their pay, beginning with those who came last and ending with the first." Those who had started work an hour before sunset came forward, and were paid the full day's wage. When it was the turn of the men who had come first, they expected something extra, but were paid the same amount as the others. As they took it, they grumbled at their employer: "These late-comers have done only one hour's work, yet you have put them on a level with us, who have sweated the whole day long in the blazing sun!" The owner turned to one of them and said, "My friend, I am not being unfair to you. You agreed on the usual wage for the day, did you not? Take your pay and go home. I choose to pay the last man the same as you. Surely I am free to do what I like with my own money. Why be jealous because I am kind?" Thus will the last be first, and the first last.

Activities

Reading

1 At the end, the landowner argues that he has treated all the workers fairly. On what is his argument based?

Speaking and listening

2 'The message of this story is a dangerous one. It suggests that there is no point in working hard or even being good, as we will all get the same reward anyway.' Discuss this opinion about the parable of the vineyard labourers.

Language study

3 This translation of the Bible does not group the text into paragraphs. Use a photocopy of the text and mark in the points where you would begin new paragraphs. Think about:
   ● shifts in time and setting
   ● the layout of dialogue.

Writing

4 Moral and religious teachers have always taught important lessons through stories and parables. Plan and write a short tale that demonstrates a moral or religious message and that could be read or told in a school assembly.

5 Take one famous parable (for example, the good Samaritan) and write a playscript of a modern version of that story. Use a setting that is easily recognized by an audience today.

Further reading

You might like to read the parable of the good Samaritan in Luke Chapter 10, verses 29–37.

from *Julius Caesar*

William Shakespeare

In this scene from Shakespeare's drama, Cassius tells two
stories about his friend, Caesar, to make a political point.

I was born free as Caesar; so were you:
We both have fed as well, and we can both
Endure the winter's cold as well as he:
For once, upon a raw and gusty day,
The troubled Tiber chafing with her shores,
Caesar said to me, "Darest thou, Cassius, now
Leap in with me into this angry flood,
And swim to yonder point?" Upon the word,
Accoutred[1] as I was, I plunged in
And bade him follow; so indeed he did.
The torrent roar'd, and we did buffet it
With lusty sinews, throwing it aside
And stemming it with hearts of controversy;[2]
But ere we could arrive the point proposed,
Caesar cried, "Help me, Cassius, or I sink!"
I, as Aeneas, our great ancestor,
Did from the flames of Troy upon his shoulder
The old Anchises bear, so from the waves of Tiber
Did I the tired Caesar. And this man
Is now become a god, and Cassius is
A wretched creature and must bend his body,

---

[1] *accoutred:* dressed
[2] *controversy:* competition

If Caesar carelessly but nod on him.
He had a fever when he was in Spain,
And when the fit was on him, I did mark
How he did shake: 'tis true, this god did shake;
His coward lips did from their colour fly,
And that same eye whose bend doth awe the world
Did lose his lustre: I did hear him groan:
Ay, and that tongue of his that bade the Romans
Mark him and write his speeches in their books,
Alas, it cried, "Give me some drink, Titinius,"
As a sick girl. Ye gods, it doth amaze me
A man of such a feeble temper should
So get the start of the majestic world
And bear the palm alone.

Activities

Reading

I Choose the most appropriate answer for the following statement.
   Cassius's purpose for telling this story is to prove that:
   ● Cassius should be made Emperor.
   ● Caesar has no more right than anyone else to be Emperor.
   ● Cassius is a better swimmer than Caesar.

2 Which parts of the stories might be exaggerated or even untrue?

Language study

3 Cassius refers to the 'tired Caesar'. What other words and phrases does he use to imply that Caesar is not strong?

Speaking and listening

4 The tabloid newspapers, chat shows and radio presenters love to uncover the weaknesses and mistakes of the rich and famous. As a pair, try and list famous personalities who have been disgraced or exposed by the media.

5 Use this information and your own ideas to hold a debate on the subject: 'This house believes the private lives of the rich and famous should be allowed to remain private.'

6 Work with a partner to prepare a short sequence for a television current affairs programme of the time. The programme is looking at the chances of Caesar being crowned Emperor and a presenter is interviewing Cassius as a friend and political colleague. The interviewer will need to ask questions about Caesar's personal qualities, while Cassius will need to consider if and how he will share his private doubts about Caesar.

Writing

7 Select one of the stories from this section and try rewriting it for a younger audience of children, aged five to seven. Don't forget to keep vocabulary easy and sentences should be either simple or compound.

8 When you have finished, work in a group with each person reading their version aloud, then discuss which you feel is most successful. Be prepared to explain your choice.

Modern Day Myths

"You'll never believe this. It actually happened to a friend of a friend ..."

In the Back Seat

Kevin Crossley-Holland

Kevin Crossley-Holland (born 1941) is an author and poet whose work is mostly concerned with retelling and translating ancient folktales, myths and legends. However, in this short tale he handles a popular modern myth.

ABBY'S my best friend and this happened to her sister, and Abby told me about it, so I know it's true.

Her sister's eighteen and she's got a car, and she's called Rachel. Last week, well, she went to a late night party. Somewhere in town, I don't know where exactly, and it ended very late. About two o'clock.

By the time Rachel drove home, the city was all empty. That's spooky! Anyhow, Rachel got going and she looked in the mirror, and there was this truck kind-of-thing, right behind her. She could see the driver, and he was big and leaning forward and well ... he started flashing her: headlights, dipped lights, no lights. No lights in the dark, that's really dangerous. Well, the man kept flashing her and Rachel didn't know what to do. She just drove as fast as she could. But when she turned left, the man turned left. Then Rachel turned right into Lake Street, that's where Abby lives, and this man turned right as well. He even followed her into her own driveway.

Rachel just put her hand on the horn and never took it off. In the middle of the night. Her dad woke straight up and he came rushing down to find out what was going on.

"That man!" cried Rachel. "He's been following me and flashing me right across town."

Then the driver got out of his truck kind-of-thing. He was big and he had a scar on one cheek – you could see the stitches. "Quick!" he said. "There's a man in her back seat. I flashed her every time I saw him raise the axe."

Then Abby's father yelled and just dragged Rachel out of the car. And the driver with the scar, he ripped open the back door and fell on the man hiding there.

Rain Man

Yorick Brown and Mike Flynn

FIREFIGHTERS in New Zealand were puzzled to find the charred body of a man amongst the debris of a recent forest fire. Quite why he was wearing a full scuba-diving outfit in the middle of a forest fire some 30 miles inland was far from clear ... Once the man was identified and it was determined where he had been diving, it didn't take long for investigators to come up with the answer. Firefighters had used helicopters equipped with huge scoops to collect water from the Tasman sea 32 miles away, which they dumped from a safe height on to the raging inferno. A very unlucky scuba-diver, happily gazing at schools of fish, must have been quite surprised to be suddenly scooped up from the depths, taken to the heavens and then released – only to plummet to a fiery death.

Activities

Reading

1 The first sentence of *In the Back Seat* claims that the incident happened to the sister of a friend. Why do modern myths often begin that way?

2 What did the truck driver look like? Why does the author describe the truck driver's appearance?

Language study

3 *In the Back Seat* is written to sound as if it is being told aloud. Find examples of words and phrases that are in the style of spoken language.

Speaking and listening

4 Do you know of any modern day myths or urban legends? Tell one you know – or invent one. Begin by explaining how you come to know the story – that is, your connection to the person in the tale.

Compare and contrast

5 Which of these two modern myths do you think is most likely to be true?

Further reading

You might like to read *Short* and *The Seeing Stone* by Kevin Crossley-Holland, and *The Ultimate Book of Tall Stories* by Yorick Brown and Mike Flynn.

You could also search for 'Urban Legends' or 'Modern Myths' on the internet

The Structure of Stories

This grid is a useful way of analyzing the structure of a story and for planning a story of your own.

Planning a Story

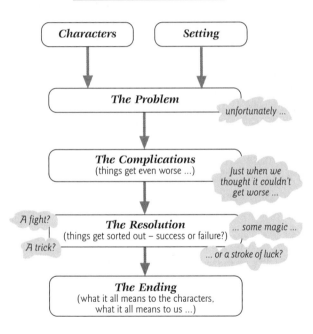

**Here are a few useful tips for the teller or
writer of stories:**

Characters

The best short stories usually focus on just one or two
characters at its centre. The hero may meet many others
along the way, but the listener or reader needs to travel that
journey with the main character/s.

The Russian folklorist Vladimir Propp analyzed a
number of traditional tales and found patterns in the
functions of plot and characters. Key character functions
that he identified were:

- Villain – fights with hero
- Donor – gives magical help to hero
- Helper – helps hero to solve tasks
- Princess – sought-after person
- King – gives difficult task
- Hero – searches for something or fights with villain
- False hero – claims to be hero but is unmasked.

Setting

The genre of your story is usually defined by its setting (for
example, a castle on a dark mountain, a space ship in a
distant galaxy, a country house, a tower block, a school,
once upon a time in a faraway land ...)

The Problem

The key to the story is the one central problem that keeps us hanging on to the end. At its simplest this might be:
- A quest to find something
- A struggle to fight an enemy (for example, good v evil, wise v foolish)
- A search for love
- Someone is trapped.

The Complications

A story should be driven by one problem but the complications might be endless. These are the features of the plot that often cause the moments of great conflict, the turning points, the comedy and the romance. Propp's analysis of stories included the following plot functions:
- The villain causes harm or injury to a member of a family
- Misfortune is made known
- The hero leaves home
- The hero is tested and receives magical help
- The hero is led to the object of the search
- The hero and villain meet in combat
- The villain is defeated
- The hero returns
- The hero is pursued
- Rescue of hero from pursuit
- The hero, unrecognized, arrives home or in a new community
- A false hero makes unfounded claims

- A challenge is given to the hero
- The task is completed
- The hero is recognised
- The false villain is exposed
- The hero is given a new appearance
- The villain is punished
- The hero is married and ascends to the throne.

The Resolution

This is often the climax of the story, the moment when justice is served or, in the case of a tragedy, when the cost of the conflict is counted. A tragedy might end with deaths (such as in *Romeo and Juliet* or *The Titanic*), whereas a comedy might end with a pairing or a wedding (as in *As You Like It* or *Four Weddings and a Funeral*). A joke or trickster tale will end with a payoff that surprises the listener. The resolution is often brought about through combat, a stroke of luck, the use of magic or a cunning plan.

The Ending

At its simplest this might just be 'happy ever after'. The final episode of a story tends to reorientate the listener/reader and show the effects of the adventure on the characters – for example, the detective back at home or in his office, the kingdom back at peace or the community coming to terms with their loss.

Activities

1 Take a story that you know well – perhaps a modern film, a traditional tale or one of the stories included in this anthology – and see how the structure of the grid above applies to it. Now look closely at the complications in that storyline and see which of Propp's plot functions apply to them.
2 Use the planning structure to plan your own stories.

Further reading

You might refer to *Morphology of the Folktale* by Vladimir Propp.

The internet is also rich in resources for modern storytellers. The simplest route is to use a search engine and enter 'stories' or 'storytelling' as your starting point. Other key words are 'folklore', 'mythology', 'folk tales' and 'fairy tales'.

Particularly interesting are the Dmoz open directory project and the Tales of Wonder site.

The website for the Society of Storytellers is for anyone interested in the art of storytelling and provides useful advice and contacts.

Activities Mapping

English Framework Objectives (Year 7/8/9)

	Page Number	Word (W) & Sentence (S) Level	Reading Text Level	Writing Text Level	Speaking & Listening
Voice					
The Pigman	13	**(7)** W18	**(7)** 6. 15	**(7)** 6, 7 **(9)** 5	**(7)** 12, 15, 16 **(8)** 10, 14, 15, 16
The Specialist	17	**(8)** S11 **(9)** S7	**(7)** 12 **(9)** 7	**(8)** 12 **(9)** 11	**(7)** 12, 15, 16, 17 **(8)** 10, 15, 16
The Genius	22		**(7)** 8, 12 **(8)** 11 **(9)** 7	**(7)** 6	**(7)** 12, 16 **(8)** 10, 15, 16 **(9)** 12
A Lady of Letters	26	**(8)** S2, 4	**(7)** 8, 14	**(7)** 6, 16 **(8)** 5, 13 **(9)** 13	**(7)** 12, 17 **(8)** 10
Paddy Cark Ha Ha Ha	31	**(7)** S11 **(8)** S2 **(9)** S7	**(7)** 8, 12 **(8)** 11 **(9)** 7	**(7)** 7, 13 **(8)** 5, 10 **(9)** 7	
Storytellers					
William's Version	41	**(7)** S7	**(7)** 8 **(8)** 3 **(9)** 3	**(7)** 2, 5 **(8)** 8	**(7)** 3, 16 **(8)** 15 **(9)** 12
Welsh Incident	45	**(7)** S6	**(7)** 8	**(7)** 6, 14 **(8)** 12 **(9)** 11	**(7)** 3, 16 **(8)** 2, 15 **(9)** 3

	Page Number	Word (W) & Sentence (S) Level	Reading Text Level	Writing Text Level	Speaking & Listening
Storytellers (continued)					
A Kestrel for a Knave	50	(8) S11	(7) 8, 12, 14	(8) 6 (9) 16	
I Shot the Sheriff	53	(8) W11	(7) 8 (8) 11, 14 (9) 6, 7, 9		
The Shah of Blah	58	(7) S2	(7) 8, 12 (8) 14	(7) 6, 7 (8) 5, 7	
Lies					
The Open Window	65		(7) 6, 8 (8) 11 (9) 7, 9	(7) 11, 14 (8) 5, 11 (9) 11, 17	(7) 13 (8) 7
This Lime Tree Bower	68	(8) S2 (9) S7	(7) 8, 12, 14	(7) 5, 14 (9) 11	(7) 2 (8) 2
The Tulip Touch	72	(9) S7	(7) 8, 12	(7) 14, 17 (8) 12, 15 (9) 15	(7) 12, 15, 16, 17 (8) 10, 14, 15, 16 (9) 12
Suspense					
The Monkey's Paw	90	(7) S18 (8) S13 (9) S11	(7) 8, 12 (8) 10, 11, 14 (9) 7, 9	(7) 5, 11 (8) 12 (9) 5	(7) 2, 12 (8) 2, 10
The Son Murdered by his Parents	93	(7) W20 (9) W8	(7) 7, 12 (8) 10	(7) 3, 5	(7) 2, 3 (8) 2
Late	96	(8) W11 (9) S7	(7) 6, 8, 14	(7) 11 (8) 12 (9) 11	(7) 12 (8) 10

	Page Number	Word (W) & Sentence (S) Level	Reading Text Level	Writing Text Level	Speaking & Listening
Suspense *(continued)*					
An Arrest	100	(7) S1 (8) S2	(7) 8 (8) 16 (9) 15	(7) 11, 14	(7) 12 (8) 10
Reported Horror					
King Oedipus	106		(7) 12, 14, 20 (8) 14 (9) 15	(7) 18 (8) 16 (9) 16	(7) 12 (8) 10
Twenty Four Hours	110	(8) S2	(7) 8, 12, 14 (8) 11 (9) 7, 9	(7) 19 (8) 18 (9) 16, 17	
A Twist in the Tale					
The Goat and the Ass	112		(7) 6, 12 (8) 14	(7) 1, 5 (8) 8	
The Huntsman	115		(7) 8, 14, 15	(7) 5	(7) 16, 17 (8) 16 (9) 12
The Happy Man's Shirt	119	(9) S1	(7) 6, 8 (8) 11 (9) 7, 9	(7) 6 (8) 8	(7) 12, 15, 16 (8) 8, 10, 14, 15, 16 (9) 12
Bottles	122	(8) S4	(7) 6, 12	(7) 5, 7, 8 (8) 5	(7) 2, 3, 12 (8) 2, 10
An Aeroplane Journey	125		(7) 12, 15	(7) 7 (8) 5 (9) 5	(7) 12 (8) 10
Three Trickster Tales	130	(9) S7	(7) 6 (8) 14	(7) 5, 7, 16 (8) 13 (9) 5, 13	(7) 12 (8) 10

	Page Number	Word (W) & Sentence (S) Level	Reading Text Level	Writing Text Level	Speaking & Listening
Magical Tales					
The Fisherman and the Jinnee	139	**(7)** S18 **(8)** S13 **(9)** S11	**(7)** 12, 14 **(8)** 11, 14 **(9)** 7, 9	**(7)** 18 **(8)** 8, 16, 17 **(9)** 16, 17	**(7)** 12 **(8)** 10, 16
Urashima and the Turtle					
The Moral of the Story					
Samurai and Hakuin	142	**(9)** W7	**(7)** 8	**(7)** 6 **(8)** 5	**(7)** 1, 7, 15 **(8)** 5, 7, 14, 15 **(9)** 3, 12
Parable of the Vineyard Labourers	145	**(7)** S8 **(8)** S6		**(8)** 8	**(7)** 12 **(8)** 10
Julius Caesar	148	**(9)** W7	**(7)** 12	**(8)** 2	**(7)** 3, 12, 16 **(8)** 10, 14, 15 **(9)** 9, 12
Modern Day Myths					
In the Back Seat	152	**(7)** S16	**(8)** 14		**(7)** 2 **(8)** 2
Rain Man					
The Structure of Stories					
	157		**(7)** 7 **(8)** 10	**(7)** 5 **(8)** 1 **(9)** 5	

Acknowledgements

The publishers have made every effort to trace the copyright holders, but if they have inadvertently overlooked any, they will be pleased to make the necessary arrangements at the first opportunity.

Extract from *The Pigman* by Paul Zindel published by Red Fox. Used by permission of The Random House Group Limited; Extract from *The Specialist* by Charles Sale, published by Putnam & Co 1930; Extract from *My Oedipus Complex and Other Stories* by Frank O'Connor, published by Penguin 1963. Copyright © Frank O'Connor 1963. Reprinted by permission of Peters Fraser & Dunlop on behalf of Frank O'Connor; Extract from *Talking Heads* by Alan Bennett, published by BBC Worldwide. Reprinted with permission; Extract from *Nothing To Be Afraid Of* by Jan Mark (Kestrel 1980) Copyright © Jan Mark, 1977, 1980. Reprinted by permission of Penguin Books Limited; Extract from *Paddy Clark Ha Ha Ha* by Roddy Doyle published by Secker & Warburg. Used by permission of The Random House Group Limited; 'Welsh Incident' by Robert Graves from *Complete Poems* published by Carcanet Press Limited. Reprinted by permission of the publishers; Extract from *A Kestrel for a Knave* by Barry Hines, published by Penguin in 1968. Copyright © Barry Hines. Reprinted by permission of Penguin Books Limited; 'I Shot The Sheriff' (Marley). Lyrics reprinted by permission of Fifty-Six Hope Road Music Limited/Odnil Music Limited/Blue Mountain Music Ltd. All rights for the world administered by Rykomusic Ltd; Extract from *Haroun and the Sea of Stories* by Salman Rushdie (Granta/Penguin Books, 1990) Copyright © Salman Rushdie, 1990. Reprinted by permission of Penguin Books Limited; Extract from *The Lime-Tree Bower* from *McPherson: Four Plays* by Conor McPherson, Nick Hern Books 1996. Copyright © 1996 Conor McPherson. CAUTION: Amateur Performing Rights apply to Nick Hern Books, The Glasshouse, 49a Goldhawk Road, London W12 8QP, England fax: 44 0208 735 0250 email infonickhernbooks.demon.co.uk Professional performing Rights Nick Martston, the Curtis Brown Group, 4th Floor, Haymarket House, 28–29 Haymarket, London SW1Y 4SP. No performance may take place until a licence has been obtained; Extract from *The Tulip Touch* by Anne Fine, published by Hamish Hamilton. Reprinted by permission of David Higham Associates Limited; *The Monkey's Paw* (1902) from *The Lady of the Barge* (1906 6th ed) London and New York Harper & Brothers, Publishers. By W.W. Jacobs; Extract from *Folktales of England* edited by Katharine M. Briggs and Ruth L. Tongue, Routledge, Kegan Paul 1966. Reprinted by permission of the publishers; 'Late' by Carol Ann Duffy from *Meeting Midnight* published by Faber and Faber Limited. Reprinted by permission of the publishers; Extract from 'Oedipus the King' by Sophocles, from *Three Theban Plays* by Sophocles, translated by Robert Fagles, copyright © 1982 by Robert Fagles. Used by permission of Viking Penguin, a division of Penguin Putnam Inc; Extract from *Twenty Four Hours* by Margaret Mahy, published by HarperCollins Publishers. Reprinted by

permission of HarperCollins Publishers Limited. © Margaret Mahy; 'The Huntsman' by
Edward Lowbury, from *Selected and New Poems* 1935–1989 published by
Hippopotamus Press. Reprinted by permission of the publishers; Extract from Italian
Folktales selected and retold by Italo Calvino, translated by George Martin (Penguin
Books 1982, first published in Italy by Giulio Einaudi Editore, SpA as Fiabre Italiane
1956) copyright © Giulio Einaudi Editore, SpA, 1956. This translation copyright ©
Harcourt Brace Jovanich, Inc, 1980 reprinted by permission of Penguin Books Limited;
Extract from *The Happy Man's Shirt* from *Italian Folktales* retold by Italo Calvino 1956;
'The Bottles' by David Greygoose from *The Works* published by Macmillan. Reprinted
by permission of the author; Extract from *Beyond Our Kennel* by John Hegley,
published by Methuen Publishers Limited. Reprinted by permission of the publishers;
Extract from *The Fisherman and the Jinnee* from *The Thousand and one Nights*
translated by N.J. Darwood, Penguin 1955, 1973 and 1985. Reprinted by permission of
Penguin Books Limited; Extract from *The Illustrated Book of Fairy Tales* retold by Neil
Philip, published by Dorling Kindersley. Reprinted by permission of the publishers;
Extract adapted from *Doorways to the Soul: Fifty-Two Wisdom Tales from Around the
World* by Elisa Pearmain, Cleveland: Pilgrim Press 1998. Reprinted by permission of the
author; Extract from *The New English Bible* © Oxford University Press and Cambridge
University Press 1961, 1970. Reprinted by permission of Cambridge University Press;
'In The Back Seat' from *Short* by Kevin Crossley-Holland, published by Oxford
University Press. Reprinted by permission of the publishers; 'Rain Man' from *The
Ultimate Book of Tall Stories* by Yanick Brown and Mick Flynn, published by Carlton
Books. Rerpinted by permission of the publishers Carlton Books Limited

Other titles in the series that you might enjoy:

Miles Ahead: A *Cascades* collection of travel writing
ED. WENDY COOLING

This selection of the most entertaining and inspiring travel writing has been edited by Wendy Cooling, widely known in schools for her work as a literary consultant.

ISBN 000 711 259 9

As it Happens: A *Cascades* collection of Reportage
ED. ROSY BORDER

Fascinating and occasionally unbelievable first-hand accounts of great events, terrible situations and epic discoveries, selected by an experienced author and former journalist.

ISBN 000 711 364 1

War Stories: A *Cascades* collection of fiction and non-fiction
ED. CHRISTOPHER MARTIN

This collection, from the author of the bestselling *War Poems*, features accounts of war and its impact on human lives from before and after 1914, written by men and women.

ISBN 000 711 485 0

Wild World: A *Cascades* collection of non-fiction
ED. ANNE GATTI

The natural world and the amazing field of scientific discovery have led to some powerful and influential writing over the years. This accessible and stimulating collection ranges from Darwin to Attenborough.   ISBN 000 711 166 5

Very Like a Whale: A *Cascades* collection of non-fiction science writing
ED. JOHN MANNION

This unique collection introduces pupils to a fascinating, but hard to resource, area of non-fiction. The wide ranging selection includes science writing from Galileo to Stephen Hawking.   ISBN 000 713 502 5

I Spy: A *Cascades* collection of personal records and viewpoints on society
ED. JOHN MANNION

A fascinating collection showing the different ways in which writers have viewed the world we live in. John Mannion's anthology includes thought-provoking writing from authors as diverse as James Boswell, Gerald Durrell, Flora Thompson and Dorothy Wordsworth.   ISBN 000 713 503 3

For further information call 0870 0100442
fax 0141 306 3750
website: www.CollinsEducation.com